STOCK MARKET INVESTING FOR BEGINNERS

How to Make Money Investing in Stocks & Day Trading, Fundamentals to Successfully Become a Stock Market Pro and Make Passive Income in Less Than 24 Hours

By
James Ericson

TABLE OF CONTETNS

INTRODUCTION

Congratulations on beginning your journey toward wealth and a secure retirement!

For those of us who have lived through the 2008 stock market crash and the Great Recession, many have become a little leery about stock market investing. And with good reason – the risk of collapse is real. However, the reality is the stock market still represents the best place to invest your money. There are several reasons:

- Over the long-term, the trend is always up.
- Returns on the stock market consistently beat those from other investments.
- Nobody who sticks it out and rides out the downturns has failed as an investor.

The long-term trend of the stock market is so consistent that it's practically a rule. That means if you're looking to grow your wealth and retirement funds, the stock market remains the best place to do so – and today, it's never been easier for the individual investor. In this book, we're going to explain what the stock market is and explore how to invest your money and what you can expect. We're going to cover the following topics in this book:

- An introduction to the stock market and investing
- Different types of investing
- Is the stock market worth it?
- Mutual funds
- Stocks in depth
- Stock investment strategies
- Exchange traded funds
- Common mistakes
- International investing
- Bonds and government securities
- Playing it safe with banking

- The investors' mindset
- Retirement vehicles
- Advanced investment techniques
- How to invest large sums of money

Let's get started with an introduction to the stock market.

CHAPTER 1
An Introduction To Markets And Investing

If you're reading this book, then you have at least some vague idea about what the stock market is. Maybe you have a 401k plan at work, and maybe you've even owned a few stocks. But to get the most out of investing, we can return to that old but true cliché – knowledge is power. If you really understand what the stock market is, then you'll be a better investor and get better results. In this chapter, we'll have a look behind the curtain to see what the stock market is all about and how it came to be. Let's begin by examining the idea of a corporation, a special kind of business that is common yet not very well understood by a lot of people.

What is a corporation

Everyone has a common sense notion of what a business is. It's an organization put together to sell a product or service and in the process make a profit. The corner mom & pop store and Walmart are both businesses, but one is small, and one is huge. Aside from the difference in size, many people don't really understand how they are different and similar. For example, the mom & pop store might be selling many of the same products that Walmart does. And yet, they might be organized very differently – aside from the obvious difference in size and revenues. Or they might even be organized in a similar fashion even though the similarities aren't immediately apparent.

The main concern here is the legal structure of the company. Please note that for the sake of simplicity, we will use definitions that exist in the United States, but other countries usually follow something fairly similar. There are several different ways that a company can be organized. Going from simple to complex these are:

- Sole proprietorship
- General partnership
- LLC (limited liability company)

- S-Corporation
- C- Corporation
- Public corporation

A sole proprietorship is often how businesses start. This is a small business set up by a single person. Often this type of business will remain a single person and is utilized for activities like consulting or doing jobs in the "gig" economy. Or it could take the form of the "mom & pop" store described above. With a business like this, the ownership is personal and so are the risks. The owner reports all expenses and profits on their personal tax return. For the operation of the business, they answer to nobody – but there is a downside. Setting up a business like this opens up the owner to liability risks. If something happens that gets the business in trouble, such as a customer slipping on some ice outside, and they slip and break their risk and decide to sue – the owner is personally liable. If the business goes bankrupt, the owner is responsible for the debts. If the owner does not have enough financial resources elsewhere to cover the debts, then the owner will also go bankrupt.

Of course, it's often the case that two or more people join up to form a small business. When people decide to set up a business like this casually but without any formal legal structure (other than contracts they agree to amongst themselves), it's not much different than a sole proprietorship as far as the legal structure. The business owners may agree to different shares of income and responsibility and set up a decision hierarchy in the business, but they will still handle taxes (and face liabilities) associated with the business on a personal level. In this case, just like we described above, if the business goes bankrupt or gets sued, then the owners are responsible for the debts.

Of course, many people who decide to start a business want to keep it separate from their personal activities, financially and legally. The simplest way to do this is to form a limited liability company or LLC. In this case, the owners are not personally liable for any debts or liabilities incurred by the business. However, this type of company operates as a "hybrid" model, and it retains many aspects of an ordinary sole proprietorship or partnership. An LLC has so-called "Flow through" taxation, meaning the profits from the business go to the owners in their respective shares and the owners pay taxes. The LLC doesn't pay tax. Taxes on profits are determined on the owners' individual tax returns, and they pay the tax. An LLC has to be formally created by filing forms and a small fee in the state where it's created. If the company gets in trouble by failing to pay its debts, for example, then the company rather than the individual owner is liable (assuming the company has everything in order, legally speaking). An LLC is a relatively simple arrangement while protecting the owners from losing everything to debt or lawsuits based on the activities of the company. It can have as few as one owner or multiple owners including corporations. While most types of businesses can form an LLC, banks and insurance companies cannot be LLCs.

Any of the foregoing businesses could have investors, but they do not have public investors. The only investment would be using private contractual arrangements.

The next level up is the corporation. A corporation is a step up from an LLC, and it's considered to be a "person" in legal matters. A corporation can do many things a person can do, such as own property, make contracts, take on debt, get sued or initiate lawsuits. A corporation can also be required to pay fines or be forced out of existence.

A single person can form a corporation, or multiple people (or even another corporation) can come together to create a corporation. A corporation is formed by applying to a state for a charter. A corporation can be a government entity, but for our purposes, we're interested in private corporations which can be for-profit or non-profit (formally designated as a not for profit).

Ownership of an ordinary business corporation is determined by stock (also described as equity). A share of stock is an ownership share of the business. We could form a small corporation between three people, John, Sally, and Trevor. As part of the formation of the corporation, it would issue shares of stock. When a corporation applies for a charter with the state, they must specify the number of shares that it will issue. For our example, let's say it issues 100,000 shares of stock. It can then issue them as it pleases, so let us say John gets 50,000 shares, Sally gets 30,000 shares, and Trevor gets the remaining 20,000 shares. That means that John is 50% owner of the company, with Sally and John owning 30% and 20% respectively. When the company makes a profit that is distributed John will get 50% of the profits. People who invest in a corporation receive certificates of stock showing their shares in the company.

These stockholders, or owners of the company, can meet and choose a board of directors for the corporation. Votes are proportional to shares of stock. So continuing our example, if the company agreed upon 10 votes, John's vote would count for five votes while Sally and Trevor would get 3 and 2 votes respectively. The directors choose the officers of the company and set their salaries and layout corporate duties.

In very small companies, the stockholders, board of directors, and officers are usually the same people or even one single person. In larger companies, the officers may also be stockholders or directors, but you can have outsiders be the board of directors, and they may hire people from the outside to be the officers of the company because they may bring in skills and talents that are useful. In that case, officers may hold little or even no stock in the company and be compensated by salary.

Small stockholders who play an active role can gain power by getting a large number of other stockholders to give them their vote on issues facing the corporation. When this is done, it's called "proxy."

Stocks are transferable. This allows the corporation to continue in existence even if people leave the ownership of the company. Returning to our example, suppose Sally is tired of the corporation, sees no future in it, and is tired of the bickering between John and

Trevor. She can sell her shares of stock to a third party which we'll call Mary, who will assume Sally's 30% ownership share of the business. Sally and Mary, if this is a private corporation, can agree on a sales price that might be based on a 30% share of profit earned by the company over a given time period, or it could be based on perceived potential earnings if it's a new venture or the company has an asset that could have potential earnings in the future. An outright sale isn't the only possibility. John, for example, could decide to sell 20,000 of his 50,000 shares to a third party, which could be an outsider or he could sell them to one of the other investors (Sally or Trevor).

Like an LLC, if the corporation owes money, is fined, or gets in some other type of trouble, the owners are not in general liable in any way, and the debts belong to the corporation. Taxes are a different matter. Depending on the type of corporation (more on that in a minute) it will be liable for taxes and fees. The corporation will pay those and the stockholders are not personally liable for them, even for taxes on profits. Stockholders are only liable for profits that are distributed to them by the company. Those profits are treated differently and not as ordinary income; the way income would be considered for a sole proprietorship, partnership, or LLC.

There are different kinds of stocks. The most important type is called Common Stock. This type of stock is an ownership share in the corporation, the type we discussed above. A corporation may also issue preferred stock, which provides additional benefits over and above common stock. For example, preferred stockholders may have a prior claim on the assets of a company. So if the company dissolves, the preferred stockholders will be able to claim ownership of those assets before anyone else. They can also receive other benefits, such as payment of fixed dividends before others can receive them. Preferred stock comes with a price, however. For example, preferred stockholders may not have voting privileges.

So far we've discussed the structure of private companies. A private company is privately held. You can't just go invest in it unless you are asked to invest (for example the company is seeking capital from outsiders) or are in the inside circle (family, one of the founders, friends of the founders). Many private companies get quite large and are even worth billions of dollars.

A public company, in contrast, has stocks that are traded on a public exchange. The activities of the company and its structure are more closely regulated by government agencies. Any member of the public can in principle buy stock in the company. Public companies are governed by reporting requirements, which force them to file public reports detailing their profits, losses, and other activities. A public company traded on the stock exchange is required to file publicly available quarterly profit and loss reports called "form 10-Q". Form 10-Q reports can be accessed online via the EDGAR database maintained by the U.S. Securities and Exchange Commission (SEC). The link for this is:

https://www.sec.gov/edgar/searchedgar/companysearch.html

Public corporations must also file annual reports, which are called form 10-K, which give a detailed description of the company's performance for the previous year.

They can also access "public markets" (like stock exchanges) to raise capital, while private companies cannot.

A stock market or stock exchange is a public market that exists for the purpose of buying and selling of stocks in public corporations. Stock markets are a vital part of the economy, that is, when considering a healthy and growing capitalistic economy because they give a company access to large amounts of capital from the public. A publicly-traded company can raise a great deal more capital than a private company can, and while private companies can get quite large, publicly traded companies tend to be much larger.

What is a stock

Stock is the capital raised by a corporation through the issuance of *shares*. The stock or capital is divided up into equal parts or shares.

Each share represents fractional ownership of the corporation. A private corporation can define the value of a share. For example, suppose the corporation has $100,000 in capital. It could issue 1,000 shares worth $100 each. If an investor buys five shares, they own $500 worth of stock, giving them a 0.5% ownership stake in the company. A *shareholder* is someone who owns shares of stock in the company.

For a publicly traded company, the value of a share is determined by the markets. The value of a share of stock in a publicly traded company fluctuates on a constant basis when the markets are open.

So, in a nutshell, when a company needs to raise money, it issues shares. The company can use the money raised for whatever purpose it deems fit, and it is not under obligation to pay the money back. Instead, the shares can be bought and sold to other individuals (or institutions) on the markets. The company may pay out proportions of its profits as dividends, but whether or not it pays dividends and how much is solely at the discretion of the company, and many modern corporations don't pay dividends.

Types of stock

We've already touched on the different types of stock.

Common stock is the basic type of stock. When "stock" is being discussed although the word "common" isn't used as a designation, it is most likely common stock to which people are referring. A share of common stock represents fractional ownership of the company. A share of common stock is also a claim on that proportion of profits, which are paid out as dividends, although not all publicly traded companies issue dividends. Owners of common stock get "variable" dividends, and this type of dividend is not guaranteed. The board of directors of a corporation can decide how much is paid out for dividends, and even if dividends are paid at all.

Preemptive rights refer to the right of a shareholder of common stock to a claim the issuance of new stock so that they can maintain their previous share of ownership. In other words, suppose that a company had 100 shares of stock and you owned 10% or 10 shares. If the company issued 100 more shares, your preemptive rights would give you the option of purchasing another 10 shares to maintain your 10% ownership stake when the company had expanded to 200 shares. Of course, you would have to *purchase* it, the new stock isn't given to you, but you're given first opportunity to take the new shares up to your current ownership percentage.

Common stock has a high rate of return when compared to other investments. However, if the company goes bankrupt and liquidates, the common shareholders are at the back of the line. Typically those who the company owes money to are paid in the following order: first creditors, then bondholders, then those who hold preferred shares of stock. Only after all of these have been paid would owners of shares of common stock be paid. Of course, this assumes that the company is even able to pay any of its debts.

While owners of common stock aren't guaranteed dividends and are the last in line when collecting on debts, they can easily be sold at a profit enabling capital gains. So for example, you might buy 100 shares for $100 in company A in one year, and then sell the shares for $250 a year later if the company has done well and the stock price has risen by $1.50 per share. The ability to earn these types of profits is why people invest in common stocks and why they form the basis of most retirement accounts (because they can gain value over time). Since the value of common stock can go down as well as up, it is called *volatile*.

Owners of common stock are able to vote for the board of directors. There is one vote awarded per share of stock. So if you buy 80,000 shares of stock in a corporation, you would have 80,000 votes.

As we mentioned above, *preferred stock* is a different class of stock that comes with some tradeoffs. Shares of preferred stock are not as volatile and lack voting rights; however, they come with two major benefits. First, a preferred stock gives you a guaranteed dividend payment. A corporation must pay a fixed dividend to shareholders of preferred stock over a fixed period of time. Another advantage of preferred stock is shareholders of preferred stock have a claim on the assets of the company. If the company goes bankrupt, after creditors and bondholders have been paid, if there is any leftover capital or assets then preferred shareholders have a claim on it before owners of common stock.

Two drawbacks of preferred stock are the following. The first is that generally preferred stock does not offer the same opportunity to take advantage of capital growth that common stock does. Second, shares of preferred stock are *callable*. This means that the company, at its own discretion, can purchase shares of preferred stock back from the shareholders. Generally, this is done at a favorable price. However, the company can take the shares back from you without prior notice, and you have no say in the matter.

Types of stock can also be further differentiated at more levels if the company so desires. The other levels may be given other powers, such as putting more voting power in with a certain class of stock. Typical definitions include Class A and Class B stocks. Class A shares have more voting rights than Class B shares. For example, a company could issue Class A shares where one share had 10 votes while a share of Class B stock would have a single vote.

Remember that a company issues shares of stock which people then buy in the markets, and the company then uses the cash. The company may or may not buy the stock back, and it's certainly not under obligation to do so. People can trade it among themselves on the market, and if an investor wants to get out, they sell their stock to a third party. So what is a stock worth? It's worth what that third party is willing to pay for it. This is what drives the daily ups and downs of individual stock prices, and when all pooled together the values of the markets themselves. You would think that the value of a stock would be set by the profits the company was actually making, but human nature being what it is that is rarely if ever the case. The value of stocks is based on hopes, beliefs about what the company may make in the future (or fears of collapse) and demand for the stock on the markets.

A brief history of investing and stock markets

We often take modern life for granted, but where does all this come from? Why is there a New York Stock Exchange?

The formation of stock exchanges arose out of a basic human need in organized societies. Some people need money for their business or project. There are other people who have money sitting around they could give out –for a price. Financial markets bring these two groups of people together.

The origins of financial markets trace back to medieval trade fairs which began around the year 1000. These trade fairs brought merchants and buyers together to trade agricultural and manufactured products. These trade fairs became "free trade zones" that were exempt from the usual taxes and duties imposed by various governments of the time.

Eventually, some trade fairs became permanent rather than happening periodically as you normally think about a "fair." One of the first trade fairs to become permanent was in Antwerp, Belgium. By forming a permanent trade fair, the notion of financial centers began taking shape. Moreover, some people at the trade fairs only traded in money, lending it out or converting currencies.

Another important development occurred during the medieval era when a concept variously called *census* or *rente* was developed. In short, this allowed people to rent or buy property using loans. The person who wanted the property would be allowed to use it in exchange for regular payments. The word *gage* is an ancient word meaning *pledge*. It's at the root of the modern term mortgage. In medieval times, a live-gage worked essentially like a mortgage, the user of the property was able to make regular payments for a specified time period, after which they seized ownership of the property. This was a great help to property owners of the time, who could then turn their illiquid property assets into cash flows.

Something that is liquid is something that is readily turned into cash.

By the 13ᵗʰ century, the city of Venice was flourishing, and also getting itself into periodic wars. Wars cost money, and so the government found novel ways to raise cash for its exploits. This would lead to the birth of the concept of tradable debt.

Basically, the government would seize a portion of wealth from the rich people of Venice, with the promise to pay interest on it. The government retained the right to pay the principal back or not pay it back as it saw fit. These deals were known as prestiti, which simply means "loan" in Italian.

The breakthrough associated with prestiti was that they could be bought and sold or traded. The value in doing so was to either sell your prestiti to someone to raise cash or to attain a guaranteed income stream by purchasing one. Essentially it would be a guaranteed income for life in the regular payments from the government.

During the interim centuries prior to the American Revolution, finance went through some shaky times due to the autocratic nature of the royal government. Kings could simply refuse to pay loans back and in some cases even jailed people who they owed money too. As a result, people who loaned money to governments often charged insane interest rates, going as high as 80% and even 100%. This was done in order to hedge the possibility the government would never pay the loan back.

This began to change with the formation of the Dutch Republic, which was one of the first examples of a stable and relatively free society. The provinces and municipalities of the Dutch Republic began paying perpetual annuities in exchange for investments. Interest rates came more in line with modern values, around 3%. The rates were low because people were virtually guaranteed that they would receive the payments, unlike the case of the harsh kings and queens mentioned earlier.

It was in the Dutch Republic that the notion of a corporation that issued stock ownership was also born. This idea began with the exploration of the globe by the sea where ships would sail out to collect "bounty" that they brought home. These were obviously very high-risk ventures, and expensive to launch. No single merchant was able to raise funds necessary to launch a voyage on his own, and so the idea of pooling money together for a commercial venture was born.

When the ship returned home, if it safely made it back, then the profits would be split up in proportions determined by the initial investment each person made.

At first, these ventures were single events. Then, in 1609, the Dutch East India Company was formed with the intent of making it a permanent and perpetual enterprise. The company received a permanent charter from the government, and it formed itself as a "joint-stock company." In other words, it allowed individuals to buy stock in the company which would entail them to a share of the company's profits.

This set off a snowball effect that has been in operation ever since. A few years later, in 1613, the Amsterdam Stock Exchange was founded, and multiple companies were formed that followed this model. In 1792 the New York Stock Exchange was founded, and by the early 19th century businesses essentially took the form of modern corporations.

People often don't know it, but different types of financial instruments or securities are traded on stock markets. In the early years of the New York Stock Exchange, government securities or treasuries formed a large part of the trading. It wasn't until around 100 years later that the volume of traded stock began exceeding the volume of bond trading on the NYSE. If you are not sure what these terms mean, don't worry as we will describe them in detail later in the book.

The importance of stock market investing

Stock market investing is important for the company and for the individual, as well as for the economy as a whole. Corporations would never be able to raise the kind of cash they do without the existence of public, regulated markets. Without companies being able to raise that cash, the economy would be much smaller and would grow at slower rates. So while you could envision a capitalist type system without financial markets where people could invest in stocks, which would be a less dynamic and far smaller economic system.

Building wealth and securing your retirement

For the individual, while investment in stocks carries with it real risks, it's largely an opportunity to build wealth. For the smartest investors, it's an opportunity to build wealth to tap in the future and so represents security in retirement. While people aren't entirely conscious of it, this is how pension funds grow wealth to pay their bills, from the pension funds people used to take advantage of when retiring from a lifetime career at a single company to pension funds used to fund public service employees. The stock market also forms the basis of 401k plans, college savings plans, annuities, and individual retirement accounts. For those who are willing to assume a small level of risk and play it smart, they represent an excellent opportunity for building individual wealth and long-term security.

CHAPTER 2
Different Types Of Investing

In the previous chapter, we learned a little bit about what stocks are and got a bit of an idea of how modern stocks and stock markets came into existence. Now, let us look at some of the different ways you can invest your money in today's world.

Preferred and Common stock

We saw in the previous chapter that shares of stock are fractional ownership shares in a corporation. Remember, the term common stock is a "common sense" idea of stock. That is, you buy a share in the company; if the value of the shares goes up, you can sell it for a profit or capital gain. You have one vote for share. You may or not may receive dividends, at the discretion of the company. And if it goes belly up, you are last in line to get paid and in truth will probably lose your money.

Preferred shares of stock are a more guarded form of investment. They are a claim on dividends but have fewer or no voting rights. They don't provide a means of capital gain, but if the company goes under you're ahead of common stock owners in line to get paid.

Some special classes of stock, class A stock, have more voting rights than class B stocks. Not all companies issue class A and B stocks.

What is a bond?

If you've looked into investing, you've probably heard the phrase "stocks and bonds." So what is a bond?

In short, a bond is a loan, made by YOU.

When you invest in a bond, you lend the money to whoever issued the bond. A bond can be issued by a corporation, so you could buy bonds issued by Apple or IBM. Or a bond can be issued by a city or even the federal government. For example, the federal government may need to raise money to fight a war. Or a city government or municipality many need money to fix roads or build a new library.

Why would you lend these people money? Because they promise to pay it back, with interest.

Generally, bonds are considered a "safe" form of investment, especially when it comes to government-issued bonds. Of course, not everyone pays their loans back. And just like a person with bad credit, a bond issuer who is viewed as risky has to offer higher interest rates. For example, Apple would probably be considered very low risk. People would be confident Apple will pay the principal back, and so Apple could offer relatively low interest rates. Your cousin Joey, however, who has a construction business is in a different boat. If he offers bonds, he'd also have to pay a higher interest rate. That would cover the risk investors are facing when buying bonds from Joey. That is, Joey may not be able to pay the principal back.

The interest rate isn't completely determined by the risk of the issuer, however. Market conditions will also have a large impact. As time goes on, interest rates go up and down depending on how things are shaping up in the overall economy.

Second, how long a bond is held has a big influence on interest rates. If you got a bond for Joey's construction company, and it was just a couple of months when he promised to return the principle – Joey might get by offering a lower interest rate than he would if it was two years before he paid his loan back. This doesn't just apply to Joey – it applies to Apple and IBM too. If Apple or IBM offers a three-year or five-year bond, they will be able to pay lower interest rates than they would on a 20- or 30-year bond. Nobody knows how Apple or IBM will be doing that far down the road, even if they still exist.

The higher the risk, the higher the interest rate that must be paid.

Of course, if you buy a bond, you don't have to keep it. You can sell it to someone else.

Bond prices depend explicitly on interest rates. The interest rate doesn't set the price of the bond in a specific manner, but interest rates and bond prices move in opposite directions. But keep in mind that the interest rate on a bond that has already been issued by the company never changes.

So imagine that in 2019 Joey issues a bond for his construction company and you buy it. It's a ten-year bond you buy for $10,000, and the interest rate is 7%.

A few years later, Joey wants to issue new bonds to raise more cash. Suppose that market conditions have changed so that interest rates have gone down to 4%.

In that case, the new bonds being issued aren't as appealing as the bond you currently hold, which pays 7% interest. An investor might prefer the higher interest rate of your bond and offer to buy it. Since it pays a higher interest rate than bonds currently issued, you can sell it for a higher price. Say for the sake of example you could sell it for $12,000.

On the other hand, if the new bonds have a higher interest rate, say 10%, then your bond isn't worth as much as the new ones. Someone could invest in a $10,000 bond from Joey and get a 10% interest rate, so why would they give you $10,000 to take over your bond that pays 7% interest? Of course, they won't. So if you needed fast cash and tried selling it, you'd have to sell it for a lower price, say $7,500.

The rule for bonds is if interest rates rise, bond prices fall. If interest rates drop, bond prices rise. Remember in this case we are talking about bonds that have already been issued and the issue is what price they would fetch on the market.

Of course, you can simply hold the bond, and collect the interest. Holding a bond for the time agreed upon is called holding a bond to *maturity*. Over the time that you hold the bond, you collect the interest payments at the rate agreed upon when you invested in the bond. At maturity, you get the *face value* back. So a $10,000 bond was purchased, you get paid $10,000 back at maturity.

How are stocks different from bonds

Stocks and bonds are totally different. A bond is a loan that you make either to a company or a government entity. If you buy a bond from a corporation, you have simply lent money to the corporation. But you don't own a share of the corporation, and at the maturity date, they will pay you back.

- A share of stock is an ownership share in a company. With a bond, you have no ownership share.
- A bond is a loan to the company (or government). At maturity, the company (or government) will pay back the loan (your investment in the bond). When you buy a stock, the company keeps the money and can keep it forever.
- Bonds and stocks can be traded on the markets.
- The price of bonds is influenced by interest rates. When interest rates go up, the value of a bond on the secondary market goes down. If interest rates go down, the value of the bond goes up.
- Stocks are not influenced by interest rates at all. The price of a stock may be influenced by the state of the overall economy, by perceptions of the company's future worth, or by a favorable or unfavorable earnings report, among other factors.
- Stocks are considered a high-risk investment. You might lose everything if the economy or the company collapses. On the other hand, you might earn a large capital gain if the stock does well.
- Bonds are considered safer investments. If you don't trade on the secondary market and hold your bond to maturity, you will get fixed interest rate payments in the meantime on a regular basis. This makes bonds appealing to retirees, and

in general, as investors get closer to retirement age, they move their investment portfolio more toward bonds.

In short, stocks and bonds are different investment vehicles. People don't usually invest in one or the other, but mix up their investments instead. If you are a risk taker, the more risk you're willing to handle, the more you're going to be invested in stocks. The more conservative you are, the more you're going to be invested in bonds which are considered more stable but with lower potential rewards.

Investing in government securities

Governments at all levels issue bonds in order to raise money. The U.S. federal government issues bonds that are called "treasuries." They come in short-term and longer-term varieties and pay different interest rates depending on the maturity date of the bond. You've probably heard of other types of bonds issued by the U.S. government such as savings bonds.

Any government can issue bonds, and frequently you will see bond questions on voting ballots. Local and state governments may issue bonds to borrow money in order to get certain projects done, such as building infrastructure. Bonds issued by cities are called municipal, or "muni" bonds and have been a safe investment as well as a tax shelter. As time goes on, however, government bonds aren't being considered as safe as they once were as cities and even states face the possibility of not being able to pay their debts.

What is a dividend

A dividend is a payout by a corporation of its profits. Dividends are not mandatory for common stock, and many companies don't pay dividends on common stock, but if you can find investments from solid companies that pay dividends, and can invest enough to make it worth it, then dividends can be equivalent to bonds in the sense of paying regular income. Unlike bonds and interest payments, however, dividends will routinely fluctuate.If the company earns more profits, then you will be paid more money in your dividends. If the company doesn't make profits, then you're out of luck. In contrast, if you invested in a bond from the company but they don't make profits, they still have to pay you the interest payment on the bond.

The Dow Jones Industrial Average

Now let us look at some common market definitions that you'll see routinely thrown around on the financial news. It's a good idea to know what they all mean. We'll start with the most famous index, which is the Dow Jones Industrial Average.

The Dow Jones Industrial Average is an index which tracks the movement of stock prices for the 30 largest publicly traded companies. It's called "industrial" because it was developed in the late 19th century when heavy industry dominated business and the markets. Today that isn't the case. Over time, the companies on the Dow Jones index change, as new growing companies knock off older companies that may be growing more slowly or even shrinking. The purpose of the index is to track the overall progress of the stock market rather than of the companies themselves.

It was created in 1896 by a man named Charles Dow, who founded the Wall Street Journal. The editorial board of the paper selected the companies added to the index. It's a price-weighted index. To see how it's calculated, we can make up a fake index of five companies. Here are the companies with their share prices:

- Acme Corporation: $50
- Beta Company: $20
- Charles Corporation: $100
- Delta Company: $10
- Excelsior: $80

To get the price-weighted index, first we sum the share prices:

$50 + $20 + $100 + $10 + $80 = $260

To get the price-weighted index, we divide by the number of companies:

Our index = \$260/5 = 52

This gives stocks with higher prices greater influence over the index. So in our fictitious example, Charles Corporation and Excelsior will have the most influence on the value of the index. This has led to a great deal of criticism of the Dow Jones because suppose those 2 companies go up in stock price while the other three fall – the heavier weight given by the higher stock prices could make the index go up, even though the overall economy might be entering a downturn because most companies are seeing their stocks drop in price.

The number of shares the company has also don't enter in the calculation, another weakness that means it may not accurately reflect the market as a whole. A big criticism is that a small company that has a high stock price can have a big influence on the value of the index.

Despite these shortcomings, the Dow Jones Industrial Average (DJIA) continues to be a widely accepted indicator of the market's health, and its value is regularly reported. The companies on the DJIA are still selected by the editorial board of the Wall Street Journal.

What is the S & P 500?

The S&P 500 tracks the largest 500 companies in the market. Since it tracks far more companies, it's a broader measure of the market than the DJIA. Moreover, to address some of the concerns people have with the DJIA, the S&P 500 tracks market capitalization rather than just share price. That is, it tracks the total value of all shares the company has issued. This eliminates the problem of having a small company that can have an outsized influence on the index by having a high stock price. Influence on the index is directly proportional to the market cap of the company. So a company that had a market cap of \$80 billion would be four times more influential on the index than a company with \$20 billion in market capitalization. In order to be in the S&P 500, a stock must be traded on the New York Stock Exchange, NASDAQ, BATS, or the Investors exchange. It cannot be an over-the-counter or "pink sheet" stock (see next section).

Other Markets

No doubt you've heard of the New York Stock Exchange, but there are other trading markets as well. The NASDAQ primarily trades in electronics or technology companies, but recently merged with OMX ABO, which is located in Sweden. Since then it also offers trading in commodities and other types of investments including derivatives.

BATS is a new exchange that is all electronic based out of Kansas, of all places. It was founded in 2005 and has been plagued by some problems including a large fine by the SEC in 2014.

Finally, we come to "pink sheets," also known as over-the-counter stocks. These are stocks issued by public companies that don't meet SEC requirements to be on a major stock exchange like the New York Stock Exchange or NASDAQ. Pink Sheets or over-the-counter stocks are low-cost investments but are very high risk. They are often priced so low that they are known as "penny stocks." In the old days, these "over the counter" stocks were traded by writing on pink paper, but today they are traded electronically. When a company is traded over the counter, it is said to "go pink." Frankly, these are dangerous investments for most people.

They go pink because they may not want to release their earning statements publicly, or they may fail to meet SEC requirements. Regulators generally consider them "ultra-risky"; however, some pink sheet stocks may be good investments. For example, new companies funded primarily by venture capitalists might be pinks. But generally, they are high risk and if you want to sell it's going to be difficult to find a buyer. While they don't qualify for NYSE or other major exchanges, there are government ratings. OTCQX designates the best pink stocks. OTCQB is monitored by the feds, and this category includes young companies that have been dependent on venture capital funding. OTC or over-the-counter ones are the lowest of the pinks and considered dangerous investments. It's the policy of this book to stay away from penny stocks/pinks/over-the-counter.

Exchange traded funds, what are they?

An exchange-traded fund is basically what its name says it is. It's a fund, so it is a "basket of assets" or several stocks or investments bundled together. You can think of it as a pool of money has been put together from a large number of investors, and it is used to buy stocks and other investment assets. Exchange traded funds can be anything, real estate, or commodities. In most cases, they are diversified holdings, for example, tracking a stock market index like the S&P 500.

However, there are exchange-traded funds for virtually any kind of investment, including bonds and gold. They are exchange traded, meaning they work exactly like stocks, and are traded on stock markets like the New York Stock Exchange. Since they trade like stocks, you can buy and sell exchange-traded funds (often denoted by the initials ETF) like any other stock, on the fly.

Investing in real estate, gold, commodities

Investing in a company is a real investment. In other words, you're providing capital to real corporations offering valuable products and services to the economy. People invest in successful companies hoping for long-term growth. Companies create value with time. For example, Apple has much more value now than it had twenty years ago before it invented the iPhone, iPad, and iWatch.

Although people talk about "investing" in real estate, gold, or other commodities, they are really *speculating*. Basically, when you're speculating, you're hoping that someone will come along in the future and offer you more for something than what you paid for it. An ounce of gold today is an ounce of gold tomorrow, it doesn't have any more intrinsic value than it ever did.

Real estate can also be speculation. For decades, people believed that the value of real estate would always increase. We found out in 2007-08 that this was not true. Believing that real estate will always increase in value is magical thinking. It might work sometimes, but it is not going to work all the time. Like buying an ounce of gold and hoping someone will pay you more for it in the future, if you're hoping to flip houses or sell for big bucks later, you're speculating.

Real estate can be an investment. For example, you can acquire multiple properties that can be used as rentals. Once the properties are paid off over the decades, then they will provide a steady stream of income.

That said, investing in real estate is really beyond the scope of this book, and we don't really consider investing in gold to be an investment at all. So our focus will remain mostly on stocks and to a lesser extent on bonds.

What is a Mutual Fund?

Like an Exchange Traded Fund or ETF, a mutual fund is a diversified group of investments wrapped up in one package. You can find mutual funds that track many of the same securities that ETFs do. For example, you can invest in mutual funds that track the S&P 500. An example is the Vanguard 500 Index Fund. You can even buy mutual funds that track the *entire* stock market, not just the S&P 500.

How is a Mutual Fund different than an ETF?

Mutual funds sound a lot like ETFs. And they are – but there is one crucial difference. Mutual funds do not trade like stocks. So they are not traded on the fly throughout the trading day. Similar to an ETF, a mutual fund is a pool of money collected from large numbers of people to put together to invest. In short, a mutual fund is a portfolio, and you're buying a share of the portfolio. Typically a mutual fund will hold hundreds of securities. Mutual funds are controlled by professional money managers. Unlike an ETF, a mutual fund only trades once per day after the markets close. We will discuss them in more detail in a future chapter.

What is an IRA and Types of IRAs

An IRA is an Individual Retirement Account. This is a type of investment account that is government sponsored and tax-deferred in some way. You can hold a wide range of investments in an IRA, such as stocks, bonds, ETFs, and mutual funds. You can also hold metals and other commodities such as gold. A traditional IRA allows an investor to invest money on a tax-deferred basis into the IRA account, where it's allowed to grow (assuming the investments will grow...). When the individual retires and begins making withdrawals from the IRA, the money is taxed when it is pulled out of the account. Any capital gains made by the investments are not taxed until they are actually withdrawn. So it can be described as invest now, tax later.

A Roth IRA is funded with after-tax dollars and will be tax-free when the money is withdrawn during retirement.

A SIMPLE IRA is a type of retirement plan that can be offered by small businesses. The business qualifies by having 100 or fewer employees.

There is also another type of IRA called a Simplified Employee Pension or SEP. These can be used by people who are self-employed.

IRA's are a large topic, and we devote an entire chapter to the details.

A brief overview of money market funds, CDs, and Banking

Perhaps the simplest type of investment is simply putting your money in the bank. At the lowest level, you could put money in a savings account. In the old days – not that long ago – when interest rates were fairly significant it was actually a good idea to put some money into a savings account. A savings account is virtually risk-free in the modern world because they are insured by the federal government up to $250,000 per bank. So if the bank fails, the government will cover the loss up to $250,000.

Even better was to put money into a CD. A CD is a Certificate of Deposit, a type of investment sold by banks. Like a savings account, a CD is basically "money in the bank" that is considered a safe investment. Savings accounts have interest rates that fluctuate with the market, the interest rates on a CD are usually fixed, although variable interest rate CDs are available. Also, while a savings account can be held for as long as you like, a CD is a fixed time investment ranging from three months to five years. Like with bonds, the time that the investment in the CD ends is called *maturity*. If you withdraw the money before the maturity date, the bank will charge you a penalty. CDs are also covered up to $250,000 by FDIC insurance.

A money-market account is a specialized type of high-interest savings account.

The final instrument related to banks we'll discuss are money market funds. These are actually a type of mutual fund. This is a mutual fund that invests in securities with short term maturity dates of 13 months or less. Colloquially, a money market fund is an investment in cash. In reality, it's an investment in highly liquid instruments, which means instruments that are either cash or could be converted to cash very quickly. It invests in cash, cash equivalent securities, and debt. It can invest in CDs. It also invests in so-called "commercial paper," which is a short-term debt issued by corporations. Similarly, they invest in short-term debt held by corporations that is guaranteed by a bank. These kinds of investments are known as "banker's acceptances." A money market fund can also invest in U.S. federal government securities called Treasuries. Finally, a money market fund will invest in "repos" or Repurchase Agreements. What this means, is you temporarily buy something from someone and they agree to buy it back at a future date. In this case, the dealer of the repo is selling U.S. treasuries to raise short term cash.

What is an annuity, are they worth it?

An annuity can be thought of as a kind of self-funded pension or even self-directed social security payments, although annuities are run by private companies and not by the government.

There are two types of annuities, *deferred annuities,* and *income annuities*. With a deferred annuity, the investor invests a sum with the company and payments are deferred until the investor decides to take them out. They are regulated by the IRS, and there is a 10% penalty for taking withdrawals from a deferred annuity before the age of 59 ½. These types of investments are run by life insurance companies and usually involve a guarantee of principle.

Funds are deposited by the investor with the life insurance company, which holds the funds with an interest rate that may be fixed for up to 10 years. After that period is over, the insurance company can adjust the interest rate once per year. Unlike banking investments, they are not FDIC insured. The funds can be taken out as a lump-sum or as guaranteed monthly payments.

An income or immediate annuity immediately begins paying out a fixed monthly payment in exchange for your investment. So you could put in $100,000 and then have $500 monthly payments delivered to you immediately, for the rest of your life. You're guaranteed a fixed sum of money that will be paid the rest of your life in monthly installments, but you lose all access to the principle. Generally, annuities are not considered to be the best use of your investment dollars directed toward your retirement, but some people will find them appealing because they offer a level of security (but remember – as 2008 showed nothing is guaranteed in life). Fixed income annuities offer security because they aren't impacted by the volatility of the market and you'll be getting that monthly check forever. You can also get an annuity that includes a cost of living increase, but you'll have to pay additional costs.

The best advice regarding annuities is to first watch for hidden fees that the life insurance company can be used to gauge you. Second, while annuities might be a good idea to boost your social security by giving you a guaranteed monthly income when you're retired, don't invest all of your money into an annuity. Also, note that your children will not inherit any leftover principle.

Risk profiles for different classes of investments

Investments of different types can be ranked by risk, although there aren't any absolute rules. But we can give a basic risk rating to each of the major types of investments we've considered. It is important to realize that to a certain degree there is a relationship between risk and reward – often higher risk also means higher potential reward. For risk, we mean losing your principal.

- Federal Government bonds: Very safe
- Corporate bonds: Safe if not classified as "junk."
- Bank CDs: Safe, up to $250,000
- Savings accounts: Safe, up to $250,000
- Money Market Funds: Safe
- Municipal bonds: Very safe
- Mutual Funds: relatively safe
- ETFs: relatively safe
- Annuity: safe, however not necessarily very good return on your investment
- Individual stocks: can have elevated risk
- Penny stocks: Extreme risk
- Investment in private companies: Extreme risk

The actual risk profile may vary on how and when you invest, but the best advice to minimize risk is to avoid putting all of your eggs in one basket, as the old saying goes. For example, there is a big difference between someone who puts $200,000 in a savings account, $300,000 in a mutual fund, $100,000 in an annuity, and $50,000 in penny stocks and a person who puts $150,000 in penny stocks and $50,000 in exchange-traded funds. Obviously, the latter person is at a much higher risk. Different people have different amounts of risk they can tolerate. The bottom line is you can tolerate the risk if you're comfortable with losing all the money. If you've only got $250,000, then losing $200,000 of it too risky investments in penny stocks and private companies is a bad idea, but only putting $30,000 in those riskier investments, and maybe catching the next "sure thing" might be a risk worth taking.

In the following chapters, we will look at various types of investments in more detail.

CHAPTER 3
Is The Stock Market Worth It?

While the stock market beckons with dreams of riches and wealth, it also puts fear in potential investors with visions of huge losses. These fearful imaginings are backed with real historical experience, mainly by the crash in 1929 that initiated the Great Depression and by the 2008 Financial Crisis, where lots of people lost a lot of money.

However, a careful examination of the stock market shows that, in reality, these fears are unfounded. The historical record demonstrates that over the long-term, the stock market experiences growth. Those who hold out during downturns – and in fact increase their investments in stocks during downturns – turn out to be the winners.

Compound interest and how it works

Compound interest is one of the most fundamental financial concepts, and yet far too many in the general public are ignorant about this crucial topic. We don't want to get involved in the mathematics here, the purpose of this book isn't to give you a headache, so we'll just review the basic concept.

You know what interest does. If you save $100 in the bank, and interest is 6%, then you'll earn $6 over the course of a year. At the end of the year, you'll have $106!

If you're not very smart, you'll give yourself a series of high fives and withdraw the $6 and buy a pizza to celebrate. The following year, if you leave the $100 in there, and the interest rate remains the same, then you'll be able to get another pizza.

But by now you've figured out that there is a better way. What if at the end of each year we simply leave the $6 in the bank? At the end of the first year, rather than calculating interest on the $100 principal, now the interest will be calculated for the $106. At the end of the second year, we'd have a little more than $112 in the bank. We've earned interest on the interest. In other words, interest has *compounded*.

An even smarter thing to do would be to put another $100 in the bank every year. If you start with $100 and put in nothing but don't take any of the earned interest out, with 6% interest every year after ten years, you'll have a bit more than $179.

Now, suppose that we go ahead and put in the $100 every year. If we were stuffing it in our mattress, saving $100 per year for ten years would give us $1,000. On the other hand, if we put it in a savings account with 6% interest and don't pull any money out, after ten years, we'll have $1,576.25.

When we are talking about $100 investments, an extra $576.25 isn't something to sneeze at over a ten-year period. In short, we've increased our principal by almost 58%, as compared to the poor fool who stuffed money in his mattress.

A bank is a safe investment. But at the time of writing, interest rates are really low. Checking you might find something around 2.4%. Some CDs might go as high as 3.1% — not very impressive numbers.

Let's say that instead of $100, you were putting $1,000 a month into bank CDs for ten years with an interest rate of 3.1% with an initial investment of $12,000. At the end of ten years, you'd have a nice nest egg of $158,770.29. Congratulations! At least you didn't blow the money. Had the interest rate been 0%, then you'd only have $132,000. So the bank basically grew the money by a little more than 19%. Of course, there is inflation too. At the time of writing, the inflation rate is around 2.2-2.5%. It's a historically low inflation rate, but with interest rates that low it's eating away at the money. Your investment is slightly better than keeping up. That's a good thing – at least you have the cash on hand. But with an interest rate on CDs that is barely above inflation, you haven't increased your purchasing power at all.

What if you invested in the stock market instead? From 1926 to 2018, the S&P 500 averaged an annual growth rate of 10%. In that case, if you followed the same investment plan of starting with $12,000, putting in $1,000 a month for ten years, at the end of the ten-year period, you'd have $241,498.21. This time, you've grown your money by 83%, outstripping inflation by a huge margin. Of course this example is a little simplistic, the S&P 500 has major fluctuations, the 10% figure is an average and you might do better or worse over any given period (in fact, in recent years, it's been around 7.7%, but that is much better than the maximum of 3.1% you're likely to find at a bank). Even so, you should see that the example is quite dramatic and unless interest rates go much higher, investing in the bank isn't a great idea. That isn't to say that you shouldn't put *some* money in the bank – you should.

Values of stocks over time

Using a real example, suppose that you started with a $12,000 investment, and invested $1,000 in the S & P 500 every month for 20 years, starting in March 1999. How much money would you have in March of 2019?

The answer is $616,704.38. The total invested or *cost basis* is $252,000. The real annualized return was 7.887%.

Your cost basis tells you how much money you'd have if you just stuffed it in the mattress. Of course, due to inflation, you've actually lost some purchasing power in that case.

If we had invested in a savings account instead, with a 2.5% interest rate, after 20 years, we would have $333,862.29. That's $282,842.09 less than if you had put it in the S&P 500. Investing in stocks is a far better deal.

TIP: The S&P 500 is a great investment vehicle that gives you immediate diversity in the world's biggest companies. Look into a

Vanguard fund or consider the SPDR Exchange Traded Fund that trades under the ticker SPY.

Case Study: What if you had invested in these three companies in 1985?

Some investments are better than others. That goes without saying. Unfortunately, one of the problems people have when investing is getting too excited and emotionally invested in one or a few companies. Then, they throw everything they have into that one company.

Let's suppose that in 1999 you invested $12,000 into the Coca Cola Company. Seems like a solid investment −after all people are always drinking coke even if they switch to the diet variety. For this example, we'll suppose that you put in the initial $12,000 but don't make any further investments, and we'll compare that and a couple of other companies including Apple (below).

In this case, after 20 years, we'd have $18,000. The annualized return for the Coca Cola Company over the period is 2.16%, and the total return is 53.3%. Basically, investing in Coca Cola in 1999 and leaving it there for 20 years would be the same as putting into a savings account at the bank.

Now let's say that instead, you invested in ExxonMobil. Sounds pretty solid right? We don't have very good electric cars yet, so nearly everyone is still buying gasoline. The same scenario – invest $12,000 in 1999 on the same day that you invested in Coca Cola.

By 2019, you've got $27,973.76 in ExxonMobil stock. That's quite an improvement over Coca Cola, where you only ended up with $18,000. But for comparison, suppose you'd invested the money in the S&P 500, without adding any additional capital. In that case, you'd end up with $54,600.27, nearly double the cash. Is that an argument for diversity in your investments? Looks to be the case.

Let's check one more company. Randomly thinking of a large corporation, how about Amazon? Actually, it's not that random because we selected that to illustrate the potential payoff from picking a high-value IPO – whose true value may not really be apparent to everyone at the time.

Amazon's IPO took place in 1997, at $18 a share. Suppose that you had invested $10,000. Twenty years later it would be worth a staggering $4.8 million. That's a return of 48,197%.

Of course, most of us aren't that far-sighted, and we miss opportunities like that, or we make huge mistakes and believe something is an opportunity of that magnitude when it isn't. Amazon's biggest competitors at the time were the bookstores Barnes & Noble and Borders (Amazon had not diversified beyond books yet). Over the same 20-year period, an investment in Barnes & Noble would have only grown by 26%. Borders, which was huge in 1997, went out of business and doesn't even exist anymore. Such is the world of capitalism. The fact is it is pretty difficult to pick winners and losers ahead of time, even if something seems like a sure thing.

Case Study: Investment in the Russell 2000

The Russell 2000 is a London based fund which invests in 2,000 small cap companies. Between 1999-2019, the annualized return on this fund was 8.55% - which is a bit higher than the S&P 500 over the same period. Had you invested $12,000 in the Russell 2000 in 1999 and invested $1,000 a month for the following 20 years, you would have ended up with $695,595.88. That's even more than you would have gotten putting everything in the S&P 500.

Of course, we're doing an exercise of looking backward, but we don't know the future. So the key is to put a little bit in the Russell 2000 (or another index) and a little bit in the S&P 500.

Case Study: Apple

Over the past 10 years, Apple has had an annualized return of 29.68%. If you had simply invested $12,000 in 2009 and left it there, today you'd have $149,592, and that is without having added an additional single penny. Not as much as Amazon over 1997-2017, but not half-bad. Remember if we invested in Coca Cola over a 20-year period, putting in $12,000, we would have ended up with just $18,000.

Other Market Indices

There are many market indices, we've mainly focused on the S & P 500 index and the Dow Jones Industrial Average, but hopefully, our discussion of those two gave you an idea of what an index is. If you're taking an index based approach toward investing, then there are several to consider (there are so many we can't possibly list a significant fraction, but we'll list our favorites). First, there are many ways we can divide up companies to make an index.

- Business sector or industry. Technology, mining, healthcare and many more.
- Asset type (say bonds vs. stocks or gold)
- Capitalization. Large company or small company, or maybe midsized?
- Location, location, location. Invest in certain regions or countries (EU or Japan, Brazil or China).

- The most general types of indices are those that track various markets or groups sizes of companies by capitalization. Some of these are:

- Amex – the American stock exchange, which was the third largest stock exchange in the United States before being acquired. It was acquired by the NYSE in 2008 and is now known as the NYSE MKT.
- The Wilshire 5000 – also known as the total market index, is a measure of all stocks traded in the United States.

- The Russell 3000 – another index that is a measure of all stocks traded in the United States. Other Russell indices measure different sized companies.
- The NASDAQ 500 – top 500 companies traded on NASDAQ.
- The NYSE Composite – an index that measures the entire collection of stocks on the New York Stock Exchange.
- The Global DOW – an index based on the 150 largest companies worldwide, companies picked by the editorial staff of the Wall Street Journal.

What are the risks faced when investing in stocks

The greatest risk you face when investing in stocks is picking one or two favorites and losing your money. Many exciting IPOs end up duds, and it is pretty hard to pick which ones those are ahead of time. We used Amazon as an example. If you were around in 1997 were you really thinking of sinking your life savings into Amazon, which at the time was just an online bookstore? That would have been pretty prescient, frankly. At the time, to most people, Amazon looked fairly solid, but nobody would have seen the massive dominance it's achieved today. Most people probably would have made equal bets on the physical bookstores it was still competing with at the time.

Of course, Amazon, and more recently Apple or Google, represent double-edged swords. Your greatest risk is completely blowing your principal. However, another risk you face is missing opportunities.

Apple is a good example of an enticing middle ground. In 2009, it was pretty clear that Apple was about to ride a major wave. It didn't generate as much growth as Amazon did over the period 1997-2017, but it sure generated enough, and any half-aware investor should have seen the growth coming. You can be forgiven for missing Amazon in the days that it was a simple website, but you can't be forgiven for missing the iPhone.

Some people play it far too safe, sticking with a long-term company that is solid, yet not going anywhere. Those that play it too safe aren't going to grow the kind of retirement income they may need.

But more often than not, the risk people face losing a lot of money. This usually results from being impatient or falling in love with a single company. We will talk more about common mistakes in a future chapter.

Ways to mitigate your risks

We'll talk about mitigating risk in Chapter 6, *An overview of stock investment strategies*. But here are some general principles:

- Don't put all your eggs in one basket. Or even a couple of baskets (don't buy stocks in a small number of companies you hand pick).
- Do massive diversification. Don't just diversify with a few stocks, diversify using indexed funds. Also diversify using different types of securities (some in stocks, some in bonds, etc.)
- Stay away from supposed "investments" that are just speculation like gold and silver.
- Only invest measured amounts in companies you think are the next "sure thing."
- Don't sell when the market is crashing. You will probably lose money.

When to get in and when to get out

You should get in when prices are low. Yes, follow the old axiom of buy-low and sell-high. The only time to get out is to do so gradually when you're taking money out during your retirement. If you can live off dividends or interest from bond payments, then there isn't even a real reason to get out of the market.

What is a buying opportunity

There are types of buying opportunities:

- During a crash, when prices that are going to rebound in the future are going for low prices.
- During an IPO, but this takes some level of luck and guesswork.

Looking at recessions and bear markets as an opportunity

How many people do you know who bailed from the stock market in 2008, or constantly talk about it now? People have an impulse to flee toward safety, and this happens with stocks as much as anything else. At the first whiff of bad news, they dump their stocks and head to the perceived safety of gold or bank accounts.

Their loss is your gain. When multiple people sell all at once – a stock market crash ensues. These aren't times to join the lemmings running off the cliff; instead, these are times to look for investment opportunities. Here is the fact that history makes clear – the market may be crashing now, but it's going to rebound, and it is going to go back up. Much further up than it went before the crash. That means a stock market crash is an opportunity. When things start sliding south, especially when they're about to hit bottom or shortly thereafter, that is the time you should be buying stocks, not stuffing money into your mattress.

In 2009, just as the U.S. was coming out of the "Great Recession," one share of the S&P 500 was worth about $832, which was down from a high of around $1,400. Now, it's worth $2,834. The time period between January 2009 and May 2009 was a great time to buy because prices were bottoming out. Had you done so, you would have basically tripled your money in ten years. The people who "played it safe" by stuffing their mattress or bank account with cash are the ones who lost out.

CHAPTER 4
Mutual Funds In Depth

A mutual fund is a professionally managed group fund that invests in a diversity of assets. It seeks to balance risk and reward carefully, and it's not a get rich quick type scheme. The more careful an investor you are and the more you would prefer having a professional manage your money, the more likely you are to seek out a mutual fund. There are downsides, however. Having a fund be actively managed means it costs money to manage the fund – so you can pay fees that can significantly eat into your investments over time. Second, there isn't solid evidence that a professionally managed fund actually does better than a diverse portfolio that isn't managed by an expert.

If you hand pick stocks, then you're going to ride on a roller coaster, with your financial identity tied to the small number of stocks that you pick. It's going to require constant analysis and possibly making judgment calls on when to abandon stocks or pick new ones. You might be forced to "cut your losses" and hope for the best. In all cases, you're constantly trying to "beat the market."

For some people, that kind of scenario won't bother them. Some folks like to dive into stocks in detail and look at the parameters that define success, stagnation, or decline for a large corporation. For others, the heightened risk and required attention isn't something they're into. If you're the latter type of person, who either wants the lower risk or you simply want to utilize an invest-and-forget-it strategy, a mutual fund might be what you're looking for.

In a mutual fund, a pool of money is created to buy stocks and other types of investments. The fund is managed by a professional money manager who does the thinking for you. The money manager is a trained professional who knows how to create a balanced portfolio that pits the right amount of risk against the right amount of caution to develop an investment vehicle that should be profitable over time. Of course, not all money managers are created equal, and some funds will perform better than others.

A key strategy used in the creation of mutual funds is diversification. That is, rather than buying stock from one, two, or three companies; a mutual fund manager will buy stocks from a wide variety of companies. For example, you could invest in a Dow Jones index that bought shares in all 30 companies that make up the DJIA. Since the DJIA basically tracks overall stock market performance, if you invested in this fund, you'd basically have shares in all the companies, and your investment would track stock market performance. And what does the DJIA do over time? It goes up. So it's a much smarter investment than gambling on one or two or even three companies. Another thing to keep in mind is that over time, companies move into and out of the DJIA, and other indices like the S&P 500. Are you smart enough to know which ones will do so over the next ten years? Probably not – so having an index fund where someone else takes care of everything for you is probably better.

The simplest definition of a mutual fund is that it's a portfolio of stocks and bonds that are actively managed by a professional money manager.

There are some differences between investing in a mutual fund and investing in stocks:

● An investment in a mutual fund is a share of a portion of a large portfolio. It may only be stocks, but it might be some combination of stocks and bonds.
● While buying common stock gives you voting rights, you gain no such rights when buying shares of a mutual fund.
● Stocks are traded throughout the day, and the price fluctuates throughout the day. Mutual funds are only traded once, after market close.

Mutual funds can be *active*, that is the manager of the fund actively picks stocks to include in the fund and decides when to buy or sell individual stocks that make up the fund. It is unclear that actively managed funds provide a clear benefit to investors. Even for a trained professional, trying to handpick winners and losers in the stock market isn't all that easy. You have to pay fees for an active fund manager as well.

A *passive* fund is not actively managed by a person picking stocks or getting rid of stocks in the portfolio. When a fund is passive, it's going to be tied to some kind of index, such as the S & P 500.

It's best to visit the website of a large company like Vanguard or Fidelity and explore the different types of funds to find out what kinds are available.

Pooled investments can make sense on a lot of levels. Mutual funds utilize diversification as a central principle. That is, instead of buying stock in one or two companies, they buy stock in hundreds of companies. That way risk is diversified – if one or two companies fail to meet performance expectations and lose value, or they even go out of business, it doesn't have much impact on the mutual fund since it consists of hundreds of companies. Risk is diluted and spread out. Besides offering the diversification, mutual funds offer the ability to invest in a wide range of securities. So you could invest in stocks, bonds, money market funds, and gold for example. You could also explore investments overseas.

A pooled investment is also one that benefits from economies of scale. The fund manager is able to buy large numbers of shares at once, something most individual investors are not going to be able to do. Because of the ability to make large scale moves in the market, mutual funds may be able to avoid transaction fees that would add up from small moves in the market. They may also have access to IPOs and other special interest investments that individual investors may not have.

Mutual funds provide ease of investment while being relatively safe investments. They also often require only small monthly commitments, so it's not necessary to invest large sums of money all at once.

Many people regard the active management provided for many mutual funds as a disadvantage. For one, actively managed funds incur higher fees, since you've got to pay the salary of the person doing the managing. Other costs related to active management such as printing marketing materials and reports on the fund's performance can add up.

Another downside involving money is "cash drag." Mutual funds must keep a large pool of cash on hand so that they can buy securities. Since we are talking about large moves on the market, the amount of cash kept on hand could be substantial. That cash is kept on reserve and so isn't available for investing. When you invest in a mutual fund, some of your money will be contributed for this purpose, meaning you're going to get less actual investment for a given dollar you put in than you would get investing on your own.

One particular risk of mutual funds is known as "dilution." In short, this means doing too much diversification in search of safety. At some point, diversifying across too many stocks might result in a situation with minimal returns or stagnation.

How mutual funds work in detail

Let's start with the word mutual. The definition of mutual is "experience or done by two or more parties...held by two or more parties for the benefit of all parties involved". From this definition, we see the first aspect of mutual funds, which is a pool of money gathered from multiple investors into a single fund for the mutual benefit of all.

Fund simply means a sum of money saved for a particular purpose. In the case of a mutual fund, the fund is saved for the purpose of investing in stocks, bonds, and other assets.

A mutual fund has some investment objective in mind. For example, one fund might focus on aggressive growth (high earnings) while another might focus on stability and regular income (think – more bonds). The professional money manager who manages the fund will select the stocks, bonds, and other investments to put into the fund to meet its specific goals. Investments are spread across a wide variety of companies, incorporating multiple business types and sectors. This is done to spread your risk and hence reduce it. Not all stocks are going to move in the same direction, and not all industries or business sectors will move in the same direction. By investing widely across businesses, industries, and sectors, we average out the risk so that the entire fund is not put in danger by the collapse of one or a few companies or a downturn in a particular sector.

A mutual fund is divided into *units*. There is a cash value assigned to a unit based on the value of the underlying investment, so units are issued to each investor in proportion to the amount of money they put into the mutual fund. The value of each unit is called the *Net Asset Value* or NAV. This is the current market value of a single unit in the funds holding. So if the total value of the fund was $100,000, and there were 100 units in the fund, the NAV would be $1,000. Investors buy units in the fund priced at the NAV. So, the number of units an investor can buy depends on both the NAV and the amount invested. So if NAV is $20 and an investor puts in $20,000, then they own 1,000 units.

Of course, it's always changing as the holdings in the portfolio rise and fall with each trading day. An important thing to remember about mutual funds as opposed to trading individual stocks or ETFs is that they only trade once a day, after closing.

It's useful to know the NAV per unit for the mutual fund. This is given by the market value of the underlying securities minus the total recurring expenses, and then you divide this number by the total number of units in the fund. Note that the number of units in the fund may not be fixed – so we need to know the number of units on a particular date.

There are two very important factors associated with mutual funds – strategy and fees. Fees are so important that we discuss them separately in the next two sections.

Basically, a mutual fund will take one of four different strategies related to growth. A general rule is the more aggressive growth, the higher the risk.

1. Aggressive growth: This is a high risk/high reward type of fund. The types of companies that are used for a fund with an aggressive growth goal include newer companies in high tech, startups, or companies in emerging markets: more risk but more potential for bigger earnings.
2. Growth and income: A more conservative approach that focuses on large-cap U.S. companies ($10 billion or more). Moderate to low risk, considered stable investments.
3. Growth: This focuses on large U.S. based companies that are growing, but companies that are smaller than those in the growth and income type fund. These are medium to large sized companies (or mid-cap to large-cap) valued between $2 billion and $10 billion. They will tend to have higher returns than those in a growth and income fund but are less stable. They are subject to be more influenced by the economy at large and will move up and down with the economy.
4. International: This type of fund focuses on large companies outside the United States. It may be fairly stable, as it focuses on well-known international companies.

Although our discussion has focused on stocks, it's important to realize that a mutual fund can also invest in bonds, cash, and money market funds. So another way to look at it is the more growth-oriented the fund, the fewer bonds and cash investments that will be in the fund. A fund can be entirely weighted toward bonds and cash investments, set up for low risk and income.

If you decide to invest in mutual funds, you'll need to do some upfront investigation. Don't just jump in feet first with the first mutual fund that you find. Look at comparable options offered by different investment companies. You'll want to seek out a fund that closely aligns with your goals, although many advisors suggest investing in multiple funds, splitting your money evenly between the four general types outlined above. If you're getting closer to retirement and are more interested in protecting your principal, then you're going to want to opt for investing in low risk, income-oriented funds. No matter what you do, check the long-term history of the fund and compare it to important benchmarks like the S & P 500. Do you want a fund that doesn't perform as well as the S&P 500? What would be the point of that? You could just invest in the S&P 500. It's a good idea to take the performance period to be at least ten years. You don't want to get suckered into buying a fund that hasn't done all that well over the long-term but had a good run the last year or two.

Fees and costs associated with mutual funds

Since a mutual fund is *actively managed,* there are going to be costs associated with it. It costs money to have someone else set up your investments, buy and sell shares on your behalf each day, provide customer support, and produce shiny reports for you to look at. These are the operating costs of the mutual fund, and they aren't going to eat them – they are going to make you pay the operating costs. So an important part of investing in mutual funds is seeking out a mutual fund that has reasonable fees.

Avoiding hidden costs and letting them eat your gains

The type of expenses we listed in the last section fall into the category called ongoing fees, sometimes known as annual operating expenses. These are the basic costs of the fund manager running their business. These fees are bundled together into a fee called the expense ratio. The industry average is 0.64% and can range from 0.5% to 1.0%. Some funds have expense ratios as high as 2.0-2.5%. If you find a fund with a large expense ratio, then you need to find out why it's high and if the fund has certain benefits that offset the higher cost. If not, it's best to look into another fund because those expenses will eat into your earnings.

For example, suppose you invested $10,000. If the expense ratio was 0.68%, then your fee that you'd pay annually would be $68. On the other hand, if it was 2.5%, then the fee would be $250. That is a significant difference. Let's use a more realistic example, comparing two funds over the course of 20 years. We will set the initial investment at $100,000. Then, we'll add an additional $5,000 each year, and assume the fund has an average growth rate of 6%. Now, we'll have a fund A, which has an expense ratio of 0.64%, and fund B, which has an expense ratio of 2.5%. At the end of the 20-year period, the expenses/fees that you would have to pay to fund B would be $115,514 higher than the expenses/fees you'd pay toward fund A – a lot of missing money that you could have used for your retirement or pay a significant expense.

You can try an online calculator for yourself here:

https://www.nerdwallet.com/blog/investing/typical-mutual-fund-expense-ratios/

How the fund charges fees may add up to extra expenses as well.

There are other fees to be aware of:

- Transaction fees – these are one time fees that are incurred when the fund manager makes a change in your investments.
- Commission fee: Charged when buying shares.
- Redemption fee: Charged when selling shares.
- Exchange fee: Charged when taking shares in one mutual fund and putting them into another.
- Account service fees: charged when you'd invested a smaller amount of money than some cutoff set by the fund.

The bottom line: small differences in fees can add up to huge amounts of money over a 20- or 30-year period, significantly cutting into your investments. Choose wisely.

Passively Managed Funds

A passively managed fund will have far lower fees, with an expense ratio on the order of 0.2%. In a passively managed fund, your money is invested in some kind of index fund like the S&P 500.

How to invest in mutual funds

The best way to invest in a mutual fund is to contact one of the larger companies that sells them. You can visit any investment company, but consider Fidelity or Vanguard and contact them about investing. If you own an individual investment account, you can also buy mutual fund shares on your own.

Stocks vs. ETF vs. Mutual Funds – Which is Right for You?

If you want to play an active, and direct role in your investments, stocks are definitely where you want to be. If you're interested in the freedom that comes with stock trading, including being your own money manager, but want the built-in diversification that comes with mutual funds, then you might be an ETF type person. If you're more safety oriented, and would prefer having a professional managing your investment portfolio, then you might be in the market for a mutual fund.

CHAPTER 5
Stocks In Depth

In this chapter, we'll talk about stocks in a little more detail. So let's recall a little bit about what we already know. Stocks are shares of ownership in a company that are issued when the company needs to raise money. If a company issues 100 shares, then one share represents a one percent ownership stake in the company. The amount in dollars that the share is worth is based on the total worth of the company. A stock is a claim on all assets owned by the company as well as a claim on future earnings.

Let's start by examining a small business to get a good feel for the principles of stock ownership. Suppose that a small company has $20,000 in cash, but they need to raise $80,000 to keep operating and expand the business. They could go for a loan, but maybe they have bad credit or simply don't want to bother with a loan and have to pay interest. So instead, they decide to sell slices of ownership shares in the company, and they issue $80,000 in stock. They are broken down into eight shares of $10,000 each. So the company is valued at $100,000, and the current owner keeps two shares for herself, and so retains a 20% ownership interest in the company.

If Bob buys one share, then he has a 10% ownership in the company, and it costs him $10,000. But suppose Betty opts to buy two shares. That means she will have to pay $20,000 but will end up with a 20% ownership stake in the company. Bob will be entitled to 10% of future earnings, while Betty will be entitled to 20% of future earnings.

If the company grows, everyone is happy. Let's say that it doubles in size a year later and is now worth $200,000. Since it's doubled in value, a single share that was originally worth $10,000 is now worth $20,000. While Bob and Betty made 10% and 20% of the earnings for the company over the past year, they don't get anything else for their shares. Saying what the share is worth is only something in reality if the shares are traded, or bought and sold. Betty's two shares are now worth $40,000. She could sell them to Steve for $40,000 and make a nice profit on her initial $20,000 investment. But if Steve isn't willing to buy them, she has to sit on the shares until she can find a buyer.

A company that doubles in size in a year has a lot of appeal to people who go around investing in businesses, so let us say that Sam comes along and buys the entire business for $500,000. That means Sam will own everything the business currently owns, including the building computers, and any business assets such as inventory or product the company sells. Sam will also be buying all of the shares of the company.

In total, there were ten shares. So $500,000/10 = $50,000 is now the price of a single share. This makes Bob and Betty very happy. Bob invested $10,000, and now he gets $50,000 from Sam in exchange for his share of ownership. Betty, who invested $20,000, gets $100,000 for her two shares and makes a nice $80,000 profit on her initial investment. Of course, she also earns a visit from the tax man.

Another scenario could be that Sam doesn't buy all the shares, but maybe he convinces Bob and Betty to sell him their shares, even if no one else wants to sell. Unless there is some prior contractual arrangement preventing this (perhaps Steve could write into the contract that he has first option to buy back shares if someone wants out), Sam could still take a controlling interest by purchasing the three shares from Bob and Betty, at a price they agree on. Then, Steve would have to answer to Sam since Steve now has two shares and Sam has three shares.

Of course, a company could also have losses. Instead, if the company drops in worth $50,000, then each share is only worth $5,000, and the best Betty can hope for is to sell her two shares for $10,000. If the company goes bankrupt, shareholders like Betty have a claim on the company's assets like computers and inventory, but creditors will be paid first.

This example of a small business outlines the general principles of stock ownership, but for large, publicly traded companies things are a little bit different. A large company is going to issue literally millions of shares, not just ten or even a thousand. To become a publicly traded company, a private one will have to meet certain regulatory requirements set by the Securities and Exchange Commission or SEC and then will have an IPO or initial public offering, where members of the public can buy shares in the company on a major stock exchange. A large amount of money will also have to be paid out to an investment bank like Goldman Sachs which will handle the IPO for the company. The company would need other professionals including attorneys and underwriters. For example, the requirements for a company to go public on the NYSE that include:

- A pre-tax income of at least $10 million for the past three years, with a minimum of $2 million each of the last two years.
- To qualify for the NYSE, the company must have at least 400 shareholders that own 100 shares or more each, and a total of 1.1 million publicly traded shares.
- The company will have to file important documents like articles of incorporation.

Where to buy and sell individual stocks

These days the best places to buy stocks are with online brokerage companies. An easy one to use is Capital One, or you can try eTrade. Online brokerages are easy for you to use from their website to manage things yourself and charge lower fees.

There are two general types of orders you should be aware of: market orders, and limit orders.

A market order is an order placed that you want to buy the stock right now and at any price. There is no price guarantee with a market order, but of course, the price is going to be close or very close to the price you see when placing the order, but it is possible that the price will change by the time you click the button and it goes through. So let us say you see a stock that is $50 a share. You place a market order for two shares, but by the time it gets processed it is now $50.10 a share. Since it's a market order, it will go through no matter what once you've clicked the button, and so you'll pay $100.20 for the two shares, even though they were $50 when you decided to buy them.

Alternatively, you can place a limit order. A limit order tells the system you want to buy a stock, but you're only willing to pay a certain price for it. For a limit order, you set the price you're willing to pay, and you won't get the shares unless the price exactly matches your limit. Using the previous example, if you set the limit at $50, but the stock keeps going up by 10 cents every hour the rest of the day, then you won't ever get the shares. You can set a limit to expire at the end of the day, or have a GTC, which means good until you cancel the order, so your limit will be hanging out there until your shares are either purchased or when you cancel the order.

To get out you can to a market stop, which is the inverse of a market order. This tells the system you want out immediately so it will sell the shares at the soonest. However, the price could change after you place your sell order and you might lose a little bit per share.

A stop-loss applies if you've already placed a market or limit order, and you can specify that you would be out of a trade if the price hits a certain value (for example you'll sell if the price of the $50 stock drops to $49).

If it's a limit stop, your shares won't sell unless there is an exact match. A limit stop could be risky – suppose that the price dropped from $50 to $48 and keeps dropping to say $20 a share – then your shares would never sell if you had placed a limit stop of $49.

Differences between public trading and private company stock example

We used the example of a small business to illustrate the general principles of stock ownership, but besides the number of shares and volume of money involved, there are a few other differences. The first is that with a public company, as discussed earlier, there may be different classes of stock. If you own common stock, you will be able to take advantage of gains in share price, but you will be in the back of the line if the company goes under and its assets are sold in bankruptcy. Those with preferred stock and creditors will come before you will. Also, while a share of common stock gives you voting rights, your voting is amongst millions of others, and the weight of your vote is proportional to the number of shares you have, and you're only voting on the board of directors. In a small business, the stockholders might have a large say in how it operates. While some large publicly traded companies may pay dividends, many do not. So you won't have the opportunity to share in earnings that you might with a small, private company.

Key Items to Look At Evaluating a Stock

Now let us look at a few key elements of a company and its stock to look at when deciding when to invest or not.

- P/E Ratio: This is the price to earnings ratio. This is an indication of what other investors are willing to pay for a stock and whether the company is "hot." For example, a P/E ratio of 15 means that investors are paying $15 for every $1 the company earns. While this is an important indicator, it can also demonstrate hype as much as saying it's a good investment.
- Dividends: A dividend is a payout of a fraction of the company's profits. If you are looking to hold an asset for the long-term, then a stock that pays dividends is something to look for. A dividend is paid out regardless of the share price, usually paid out quarterly. You can reinvest your dividends or cash them out. Dividend per share is going to be small, and so, you'll have to acquire a large amount of money to earn a lot from dividends. Some people with large amounts of shares can live off cashing out the dividends. Look at older big companies for dividends, and some pay 6%. The dividend payment might be a few cents or a dollar per share.

The dividend yield is dividend payment/price per share *100, expressed as a percentage.

- Ask Price: the price you are asked to pay when you buy a stock. Can be slightly higher than the current value of a stock. The bid price is an offer amount to buy a stock. When the bid price and ask price match, the stock is traded.
- Beta: Measures how volatile a stock has been over the past five years. If Beta is greater than 1, that is a higher risk stock that has had a lot of volatility. If Beta is less than 1, it has lower risk and not as volatile.

Definitions

Making your way around the stock market as an investor requires you to know several definitions. Of course, we've gone over a lot of investment jargon already but here is a basic list that should help new investors:

- After-Hours trading: Takes place outside normal business hours when the exchanges are open.
- Bear market: Most stocks are declining in value. They are often associated with recessions.
- Big Board: The New York Stock Exchange.
- Bid Price: A price offered by a prospective buyer for a stock. If you place a limit order, the price you've offered is your bid price.
- Blue Chip Stock: A large, well-established company. Has operated over a long-term period of many years and has a large market-capitalization in the billions, even above $10 billion. However $5 billion is generally accepted as a cutoff for blue-chip stocks, is a leader in its market sector, at least a top three company. Often a "household name," a stock does not have to pay a dividend to be a blue chip stock, but a regular dividend −especially if the dividend payments are either stable or steadily rise with time − is a good sign of a blue-chip stock. Blue chips are companies that have been around a while and shown the ability to withstand the ups and downs of the market and the economy. However, there

are no guarantees. Consider that General Motors, which had been around for a century, faced bankruptcy in 2008.

- Bull market: A time of economic expansion when most stocks are increasing in price.
- Call: An option to buy shares of a stock at a pre-arranged price. It's called an option because the buyer has the option to back out of the deal while securing the right to proceed with it if they want to. This is an agreement between a buyer and seller that will take place at some future date to trade a specific stock. A call has a set price per share that has been agreed upon on the given date, and a premium is paid to the seller. The seller cannot back out, so if the stock price has gone up by the time the sale date arrives, the seller has to sell at the pre-arranged price even if it's lower than the price per share on the markets that day. However, a call indicates confidence that the stock price will increase in the future. In other words, a call buyer will benefit if they have agreed on price $x but the stock went up to some new value $(x +y)$ by the date of the sale when the buyer gets that stock for $x.
- Discount brokers: Online brokers that provide trading at discounted prices.
- Earnings per share: This is simply the amount the company earned over the past year divided by the number of shares.
- Index: A composite representing a group of stocks. For example, we've already discussed the Dow Jones Industrial Average, Russell 2000, and S & P 500.
- Margin: This refers to borrowing money to buy stocks. The money is borrowed from the broker. Your broker will have specific requirements for you to meet to be eligible to buy stocks on the margin.
- Put: A put option is an agreement to trade a stock on a future date like a call. The seller pays the buyer a premium. The seller can choose to sell or not, and if the seller chooses not to sell, they still have to pay the buyer the premium. The contract has an expiration date, but the seller can sell the stock to the buyer before the expiration date. Like a call, this has a prearranged stock price that is set even if the price on the market has changed by the sell date. Since the price is

predetermined when the contract is agreed to, this indicates a lack of confidence about the future price of the stock.

- Portfolio: A collection of investments. It can be held by a single person or a company. Could refer to the assets held by a mutual fund.
- Quote: Current price of a stock.
- Short: With a short sale, the investor borrows a certain stock from a broker. Then, the investor sells the stock at the current price and gets the proceeds credited to their margin account (the account used for borrowing from the broker). Later, when the share price drops, the investor buys the same number of shares on the open market at the lower price. Then, they return the shares to the broker whom they originally borrowed them from. The difference in price is pocketed by the short selling investors as profit. For example, suppose you borrow 100 shares of Acme stock from the broker. Then, you sell them on the market at the current price of $100 per share. You now have $10,000. After some time goes by, the price drops to $50 per share. Now, you buy back the 100 shares for $5,000. Now, you return the 100 shares to the broker. And aside from some fees, you've made a profit of $5,000.
- Ticker symbol: The abbreviation used to represent a given stock on the exchange, for example, APPL for Apple Inc. Also used for funds, SPY is an exchange-traded fund for the S&P 500.

Keep in mind that options trading (calls and puts) and short selling are advanced activities that carry major risk.

How to choose a good stock to invest in

Knowing what a good stock is, depends on what your goals are. If you are looking for high returns, then you might be more interested in companies that have had recent IPOs that are expected to have solid long-term growth. Of course, some older companies are also growing rapidly, like Netflix. If you're looking for long-term stability and income, you can select from older, stable companies and seek out those who pay dividends. Actually knowing what stocks to pick can be a risky activity and it is not recommended for most beginning investors. Some other tips:

- Undervalued Stocks: Price to earnings ratio can indicate a hot stock people are chasing, but if the P/E ratio is 15 or lower that could indicate a lower valued stock. The stock price is relatively low for the earnings the company is generating, indicating it's a buying opportunity.
- Revenue growth: Seek out companies that have demonstrated revenue growth, and beyond the immediate short term. There are a lot of day-to-day and month-to-month fluctuations, check revenues for the past 3-5 years to see trends.
- Use balance, just like a mutual fund might. Don't put everything into one stock. Build a larger portfolio of stocks across different sectors.
- Check the news reports on the company to find out what people think about it and what its future prospects are.
- Price alone isn't a reason to buy a stock. If a stock is cheap, that doesn't mean it will gain in the future; it might even lose more value.
- Have your selling criteria ahead of time and set in stone. Don't let emotions govern your decisions, sell when a stock stops performing at a level you've set ahead of time.

CHAPTER 6
An Overview Of Stock Investment Strategies

Now let's look at some basic stock market investing strategies.

Riding gains (and losses) with individual companies

Investors with a higher tolerance for risk can buy stocks in individual companies and build their own, customized portfolio. While people intellectually approach things by examining the data and financials, those inclined to this kind of investing are also letting emotions intrude. Buying individual stocks is often something that happens based on gut-level feelings that may or may not be correct.

If you are this kind of investor, and important strategy – one echoed everywhere – is to avoid the panic impulse when stocks suffer short term declines. If you are interested in building wealth and having wealth over the long-term then riding out the losses that will inevitably be experienced is an important part of your investment strategy. Of course, some individual companies may tank, and so, it is important to know when to let go as well.

Diversification

A lot of stock market investing is built around the concept of mitigating risk. For many people, too much risk puts them off. The oldest way to mitigate risk in the markets is to diversify your portfolio. Suppose that John has invested $100,000 in three stocks:

- Apple
- Facebook
- Google

His friend Mary, however, has invested $100,000 in the following way:

- An income-oriented mutual fund
- A real estate ETF
- The S & P 500
- The Russell 2000
- The Wilshire 5000
- An international fund
- Apple
- Google
- Facebook
- Ford Motor Company
- Wells Fargo Bank
- United Healthcare

If a scandal hits (privacy violation say) and the big tech firms begin suffering stock declines, John also suffers – big time. Mary has bought stock in those companies as well so takes some losses there – but she is also well protected. Mary has taken the time to not only invest in high tech, but to invest in autos, overseas companies, banking, and healthcare. In addition, she's also protected herself by investing in several index funds and some bonds in her income-oriented mutual fund. Mary is well positioned to ride out the storm, and the overall value of her portfolio might be impacted. The losses for Apple, Google, and Facebook might be offset by gains in her other investments.

John meanwhile, loses a lot of money and panics, selling his shares at a loss.

Dollar Cost Averaging

Dollar cost averaging is a strategy that takes emotion out of investing and averages out the inevitable ups and downs that the stock market will experience. The procedure can be summarized in two steps:

- Invest a fixed amount.
- Invest at regular intervals.

If you choose to do dollar cost averaging, then it's a rule you must follow. If the market starts dropping – or whatever – you never deviate from the rule. The point of the rule is to average out those ups and downs. So for example, if we decide we want to use a $1,000 investment to buy stocks using dollar cost averaging, we can pick a specific day of each month to buy stocks. For example:

- Buy stocks on the 10th of each month.
- Buy exactly $1,000 worth.

This procedure can work with any type of investing, but it probably works best with indexed funds. Later we will discuss ETFs or exchange-traded funds. There are ETFs available for all kinds of investments and indices, but for example, you can buy an ETF for the S&P 500. So a good dollar cost averaging strategy would be to buy $5,000 worth of shares in the S&P 500 month-in and month-out. Of course, we just made up the $1,000 figure; you can do this using any amount of money, as little as $100 per month or even less. The point is to make your investments in fixed amounts, at the same time.

Dollar cost averaging eliminates the short-term volatility of the markets. It's a long-term strategy to build wealth over time. If you are doing your investing through your employer, it's easy to set up a dollar cost averaging type investment strategy with your 401k by investing a set amount each month into indexed funds. You can also use it with your own mutual funds or exchange-traded funds. In fact, you can use it with your own stock portfolio if you choose to go that route.

Another way to do dollar cost averaging is to buy a set number of shares per month if you are managing your own investing. So, for example, suppose that you have the following portfolio:

- Apple
- Microsoft
- Google
- S&P 500 index fund

- Russell 2000 index fund

We could commit as an example, to each and every month purchase:

- Two shares of Apple
- Three shares of Microsoft
- One share of Google
- One share of S&P 500
- Two shares of Russell 2000

After doing this for a year, then you own 24 shares of Apple, 36 shares of Microsoft, 12 shares of Google, 12 shares of S&P 500, and 24 shares of the Russell 2000. Doing it this way, the short term ups and downs of individual stocks won't impact you.

Long-term investment strategies

In truth, we've already reviewed some basics of long-term investment strategies. The long-term investor is not concerned with the short term ups and downs of the markets, or what's in the news. Today's recession will be tomorrow's economic boom. If a company like Apple flops a product this month, or sales don't match "expectations," chances are Apple will still be around and profitable in five years. Unless there is a very, very major problem – you should ignore what they are babbling about on the news.

The long-term investor should utilize all the strategies discussed in this chapter and a few more.

- Build a diversified portfolio.
- Invest in a Blue Chip fund as part of your overall investment strategy, to form a stable core of your portfolio.
- Invest heavily in indexed funds.
- Seek out blue-chip stocks that pay dividends.
- Don't panic when there is a market downturn – ignore the impulse to sell off.
- When there is a market downturn, start buying.

- Use a strategy based on dollar cost averaging. You really shouldn't be *thinking* about your investing very much.
- Never let emotion get in the way of your investment decisions.
- Include other non-stock investments in your portfolio. These can include bonds, US Treasuries, and cash investments including putting some money in the bank. You can even include an annuity.

Buy low, sell high

It goes without saying, but you want to buy low and sell high, probably the oldest principle in business. In the stock market, you can narrow this a bit further – you should see market crashes as opportunities. When the market starts tanking many people have the impulse to sell and move into cash or bonds. Knowing the long-term history of the market, you should be willing to ride out short term fluctuations (and even major recessions are short term fluctuations). When everyone else is selling, you should take advantage of the lower prices to grab stocks at bargain prices.

A look at the Dow Jones Industrial Average over the long-term can help set some perspective.

https://upload.wikimedia.org/wikipedia/commons/c/c8/DJIA_historical_graph_to_jul11_%28log%29.svg

Notice that while there are some short term bumps, there is one trend – it's upwards. Even the Great Depression doesn't figure much in the long-term history of the stock market.

Buying low applies at all times for all investments – if you are doing indexed funds, a stock market decline is a great time to load up on them.

If you are trading individual stocks with the hopes of building shorter-term profits, then selling high is another part of your strategy. Although it's not a good idea to guess, people have a sense when a market is peaking. You can sell at a time when you've made an acceptable profit by selling your shares. The actual value is up to you.

Knowing when to buy and when to sell

Frankly, there is no good time to sell an indexed fund unless you are in retirement and need the cash or you have an emergency. You should hold them over the long-term.

For individual stocks, you might make the wrong bets. When you see a company failing to live up to the initial promises, or if they run into trouble like Theranos, it's a good idea to get out early. If a company, say a coal company, has done well in the past but is experiencing very slow growth or stagnation and there is no long-term future, you might want to swap that stock out for a company with growth potential.

CHAPTER 7
Exchange Traded Funds

Exchange traded funds are my favorite kind of investment. You'll see why in a second. So far, we've discussed mutual funds, which represent a lower risk, controlled type of investment. Mutual funds are diversified, and it is easy to invest in mutual funds using dollar cost averaging. But, they cost money, and you have little control, which you've handed over to a money manager. Also, mutual funds only trade once a day after the market closes.

Buying stocks gives you more direct control. Rather than having a money manager you have to pay to carry out his services, including making copies at the office, paying for phones and other incidentals you probably don't like paying for, with stocks you're the one doing the trading. This has some risks, but for those who want control over their investing, it has appeal. Also, you may like the flexibility of being able to buy and sell any time the markets are open. However, due to the buying power of a large group of individuals and a money manager who is working on the markets full-time, it's hard to get the kind of diversification and other benefits that you're going to get with mutual funds.

What if you could wave a magic wand and combine the best of mutual funds with the best of stocks? Well, it turns out that you can. The result is the exchange-traded fund. When you boil everything down to basics, and the exchange-traded fund is an unmanaged mutual fund that trades like a stock.

An ETF gives you automatic diversification – its biggest advantage. Even if you don't exclusively trade in ETFs, it's a good idea to have them as a significant portion of your portfolio.

Typically, an exchange-traded fund will track some kind of stock index. There are a wide array of exchange-traded funds; they also track bonds, real estate, cash, commodities, currencies, and baskets of assets. The price of ETFs changes throughout the day as they are traded on the major stock exchanges. So buying or selling an ETF is just like buying or selling a share of Apple or General Motors.

Like with mutual funds, you may see a lot of discussion of asset classes on websites for investment firms that have created ETFs. There are five asset classes:

1. Stocks
2. Bonds
3. Money market instruments (cash)
4. Commodities
5. Real estate

In contrast to mutual funds, in addition to being able to trade them in real time rather than waiting for an end of the day settlement, many ETFs have larger volumes than mutual funds. They also have lower fees, in some cases much lower. As a result, they are a very attractive option.

For the beginning investor, ETFs are highly recommended. It's a way to get in on your own and have some protection by utilizing the built-in diversity that ETFs have. You can buy ETFs using market orders through your own online brokerage if you know the ticker symbols of the funds you want to buy. They are a great way to do individualized dollar cost averaging. You can buy shares at regular intervals as part of your investment strategy.

To get an idea of what kinds of ETFs are available on the market, you can visit the *State Street Global Advisors SPDR* site. It's located here:

https://us.spdrs.com/en

The low-cost core is the first class of ETFs we will look at. These are divided into:

- U.S. Equities
- International Equities
- Fixed Income

If you click on U.S. equities, you will see that there are several funds that have different options for tracking major parts of the stock market. For example, they have three options available for tracking the S&P 500:

- Growth
- High-Dividend
- Value

If you look under the general category for U.S. equities (not the low-cost core), you will see that you can also simply track the S&P 500 using SPY. Our friends at State Street work like a mutual fund, in the sense that they've used a large sum of money to buy stocks in the 500 companies that make up the S&P 500. You can buy small shares of it. At the time of writing, the stock is priced at about $285 per share.

However, SPYG – the S&P 500 Growth fund – is only $37 a share (prices will vary, by the time you read this). The fund also tracks the S&P 500 index but gives you a low-cost way to get in the market. However, this fund is designed to tap companies in the S&P 500 that are believed to have the most growth potential. According to the website, they base this on the revenue growth, price to earnings ratio, and momentum of the companies chosen for the index.

You can also use SPDR ETFs to invest in preferred stock or commodities. GLD allows you to buy gold shares. NANR is a natural resources fund that you can use to invest in energy, metals, mining, and agriculture. You can also invest in bonds, loans, U.S. government treasuries, and overseas investing like China or Japan.

SPDR is not the only company out there. A recent arrival on the scene is a company called Robin Hood. This company has a mobile app that can be used to trade on your smartphone or tablet. One advantage of Robin Hood is that it's commission free. It also allows you to invest in options and even cryptocurrencies, as well as directly in stocks.

https://www.robinhood.com/

Vanguard, a very popular investment firm known for mutual funds, also offers several ETF options. Their S&P 500 indexed fund VOO is one of the most popular investment options.

Another one of the big players in the ETF world is iShares by BlackRock. They are offered in four asset classes:

- Equity (stocks)
- Fixed income (bonds)
- Real estate
- Commodity

You can also invest by region:

- United States
- Europe
- Asia/Pacific
- Global

Or by market:

- Developed
- Emerging

For example, iShares offers a fund which tracks the Russell 2000. According to the website, had you invested $10,000 when the fund was started in 2000, today you've had about $40,000. The fund invests in smaller publicly traded U.S. companies that have long-term growth potential. Like investing in an S&P 500 index, this fund will give you a chance to invest simultaneously in all companies that make up the index – in this case, the 2000 small-cap companies on the Russell 2000.

If you look at the expense ratios, you see where you can get big advantages over a mutual fund. Expense ratios on iShares go as low as 0.04, with most around 0.19-0.20.

Remember these funds trade like stocks – so you don't have to enroll at iShares to buy iShares funds. You just have to know what the tickers are, and you can sign up with any brokerage firm and buy the funds as part of your everyday trades.

Note that while we've often talked about the S&P 500, you can invest in exchange-traded funds that track all markets. For example, the PowerShares QQQ fund tracks the NASDAQ 100.

The Advantages and Disadvantages

Although it's hard to say that ETFs have disadvantages, if you are person who would rather hand over control to a money manager, then an ETF is not for you because trading and investing in exchange-traded funds requires your active and direct participation, and there is no expert who is going to pick the right funds for you.

However, due to the instant and automatic diversification that exists with these types of investments, they are fairly low risk as long as you follow some basic investment common sense. The flexibility is a major advantage, but you shouldn't abuse it. In other words, when you decide to invest in a fund unless there is some very serious compelling reason to get out – stay in that fund. ETFs represent an opportunity for solid, long-term investing.

How to utilize ETFs and Where to Invest

You invest in ETFs at your regular brokerage. You should use the websites of major funds to educate yourself about what funds are on offer and what the goals are of each fund. That way you can carefully select funds that meet your own investment goals.

You can also compare funds offered by one company versus another, to examine performance. Earlier, we mentioned that iShares offered a Russell 2000 fund. SPDR also offers a small-cap fund that tracks the 2000 smallest publicly traded companies in the United States. How do the two funds compare?

- The iShares fund is larger, with 282 million outstanding shares, compared to about 40 million for the SPDR SPSM fund.
- Both have a similar P/E ratio of about 16.
- The expense ratio of the SPDR SPSM fund is 0.05%. For the iShares fund, it is 0.19%.
- The price of a share of SPSM is about $30, at the time of writing the iShares fund is $154 per share.
- Year to date, the iShares fund is up 15.8%, the SPSM fund is up 17.3%.

You might ask why the funds track the same index but don't offer the exact same performance. The reason is that each company makes its own decisions on the weight given for investments. For example, we can look at the top ten holdings of each fund. For the iShares fund we have:

- ETSY
- TRADE DESK INC-CLASS A
- FIVE BELOW INC
- CREE INC
- HUBSPOT
- PLANET FITNESS INC. CLASS A
- CIENA CORP.
- PRIMERICA INC.
- ENTEGRIS INC.
- ARRAY BIOPHARMA INC.

For SPDR's SPSM fund the top ten holdings are:

- MR. COOPER GROUP INC.
- TRADE DESK INCORPORATED CLASS A

- PLANET FITNESS CLASS A
- VERSUM MATERIALS INC.
- CREE INC.
- MELLANOX TECHNOLOGIES LTD.
- ITT
- ARRAY BIOPHARMA INC.
- COUPA SOFTWARE INC.
- INSPERITY INC.

As you can see, while there is some overlap, the different funds have given different weights to different companies, and the top ten lists then turn out different. The difference isn't all that significant, but you may note that the SPDR fund has performed a little better on a YTD basis. Over the past five years, the five-year market price of the SPDR fund has grown 7.59%, in comparison to 4.46% for the iShares fund. So the SPDR fund hasn't just done better recently, it is done better for the past five years. That coupled with its lower costs (both the share price and expense ratio) make it a more attractive option in our view. But we aren't here to advocate for one or the other, but rather to give you an idea of how you might do your own analysis with these types of funds.

The lower share price of the SPDR fund will make it more accessible for those who are starting out with a lower budget or who don't want to risk large amounts of capital.

Super Diversification with ETFs

As we stated at the beginning and illustrated by looking at a couple of funds, ETFs provide automatic diversification, the same kind you get with mutual funds but without the costs, constraints, and hassles. If you want to build a solid, really diverse portfolio consider picking your favorite ETF company and buying into all of their funds over time, or a diverse subset of them. Since there are funds that invest in stocks, bonds, real estate, and commodities, it's pretty easy to build up a portfolio that meets your investment goals, whether you're playing it safe looking for an income-based portfolio or looking for aggressive growth or some balance in between.

ETFs versus Picking Stocks

ETFs trade like stocks, but they are not investments in individual companies.

Where did ETFs come from?

The history of exchange-traded funds traces its roots back through mutual funds. The first mutual fund was developed in 1774 by a Dutch merchant. At that time, he used pooled investing to allow people to invest in a closed-end fund. A closed-end fund has a pooled amount of capital that it raises through an IPO, and it's managed by a professional money manager. In modern times, closed-end funds are publicly traded funds themselves. From 1774 until modern times, mutual funds were the only game in town when it came to index funds.

The first attempt to launch an exchange-traded fund came in the United States in the late 1980s when there was a fund indexed to the S&P 500. However, a federal judge actually struck it down, saying the fund had to be traded in futures markets. This ruling kept the fund out of the reach of ordinary investors, but soon afterward the first true exchange-traded funds were brought to market.

In 1990, an exchange-traded fund was introduced on the Toronto stock exchange in Canada, which tracked 35 large Canadian companies. This was soon followed a few years later by the creation of the S&P 500 Trust, an ETF that was created by our friends the State Street Global Advisors SPDR. This fund caught fire and remains very popular today, and as we've seen, State Street has massively expanded the funds they have available with investing possibilities in virtually every asset class and market segment, both here in the United States and globally.

At first, ETFs were primarily used by institutional investors. However, their use quickly caught on, and financial advisors and individual investors became interested in using exchange-traded funds to invest. Between 2000 and 2010, the total amount invested in ETFs grew from $0.1 trillion to $1 trillion, and by 2017 that figure had grown to $3.4 trillion.

CHAPTER 8
Common Mistakes

Now let's explore some of the common mistakes made by beginning investors. Don't let yourself get caught up in them. There are plenty of books to buy and websites to read to educate yourself on the markets.

Not understanding the markets

Not understanding the markets is the first mistake newbies often make. Before you get out your wallet or bank card, make sure that you understand the basics before you start buying. That means having a good idea what all the index funds mean, some basic stock market jargon, and knowing the different ways you can buy stock. It's also important to understand the markets on another level. That is, you should understand the history of the markets and not be another naïve fool that panics every time the DJIA goes up and down. Don't listen to the press, they concoct theories about ups and downs in the markets that could have some connection to reality, but the fact is nobody knows. All too often you hear that the market is dropping and people are unloading shares because of some news report. Are you going to be that person who unloads your shares because of a news report? If you understand the markets, then you won't be. You'll be buying extra shares instead.

Not having clear investment goals

Let's get one thing out in front – the stock market is not a get rich quick scheme. So you're not going to make a few investments and then have a big house, two luxury sports cars and oodles of time to travel.

Investing is not a gambling casino; it's a place where you invest real money into real businesses. In order to achieve success, you need to have clear investment goals. This comes from two sides, from the investment side and the end game side. For example, on the investment side the kind of goals you need to come up with are:

- What is the minimum amount you will invest?
- How frequently are you going to invest? Don't do it on the fly; have a plan. Once a month? Every two weeks? Daily? It doesn't really matter in the details, but it is important to have a plan.
- Set monthly and annual goals for the amount you will invest.

Next, you should have a clear idea of what you want to invest in. Too many people just go around not thinking very far ahead and then hear about some hot new company, "buy gold" or "invest in crypto" and then jump on the bandwagon. Impulse is not something that is good to have as a part of your investment goal bag of goodies. Instead, get a clear idea of where you want to go:

- What business sectors do you want to invest in?
- Do you want growth, income, or some combination of both?
- How much capital are you willing to put at risk?
- Do you only want to invest in the United States, or expand globally?
- What about real estate, natural resources, and commodities?

Once you've figured all this out, write down how you want to weight each item. For example, suppose that Mary decides she wants to invest in the following areas:

- Healthcare
- Technology
- An index fund
- Bonds, but looking for high income

The next thing Mary needs to do is think about what percentage of her investments she wants to devote to each of these four items. Since Mary is looking for high income from bonds, she probably wants to invest in some junk bonds that pay high interest rates. Of course, "junk" bonds suggests they may default, so there is a bit of risk there. There is also some risk for technology stocks. These days technology is changing rapidly, and today's giants might be knocked off the top by some currently unknown upstart. With that in mind, though Facebook or Apple might look secure now, you really don't know if they are going to be secure and remain market leaders in ten years, due to the sector itself being so volatile and ripe for disruption. Healthcare faces other issues. It might seem sensible to invest in large health insurance companies or health-related companies, but what if the public votes in politicians that want to install Medicare for all? That might diminish or even eliminate health insurance companies. On the other hand, if the current system stays largely in place, then investments in big health-related companies like United Healthcare make good sense. So Mary is taking a bit of a risk there too.

Since Mary has three risky investment choices, she decides to put 50% of her investments into an index fund, and she chooses an S&P 500 ETF. She then breaks up the other 50% by putting 10% into the bond investments, and then 20% each into technology and healthcare. Mary wants some security that comes with a fund like an S&P 500 ETF but also enjoys looking at individual stocks and doing her own picking, so she decides to buy stock in individual companies for healthcare and technology.

The details of this little exercise aren't really important, and rather, we simply want to illustrate how Mary has developed and executed a plan to organize her investments to get what she wants out of them. Now, she has to settle on a monetary figure that she will invest, and how often she will invest. Suppose that Mary plans to put $500 at the end of each month. Now, Mary has planned her investment strategy, and as long as she sticks to her plan, she is likely to enjoy success.

Letting emotions rather than facts govern decisions

Emotions have a nasty way of injecting themselves into stock market investing. It's exciting and can be filled with fear if you're looking at losing your shirt. Of course, the real problem is that people overestimate the dangers. In particular, people take a short term outlook. So if they are in the midst of a crash as we were in 2008, people see the stock market dropping and think it's the end of the world. We hope that we convinced you in earlier chapters that this is not the case, and those who tough it out get the most rewards. Going into a panic and wanting to sell before you think the market is going to bottom out is a naïve and emotionally based approach. Markets never bottom out and stay there.

A second area where emotions rear their ugly heads is in picking stocks. People often pick stocks on feelings rather than facts. That is not a way to generate long-term success in the markets.

Patience is a virtue

The stock market, for the most part, really is a race between the tortoise and the hare. Once you realize that you're not going to find a get rich quick scheme and begin regular, methodical investing, your patience will begin to pay off. Over the long-term, those that are patient and stick to a strategy that incorporates diversity and dollar cost averaging are sure to achieve secure retirement and financial independence.

The gullibility of the next "sure thing."

This happens all the time, but a good recent example is Theranos. The company had a charismatic female CEO and made promises of a medical breakthrough that would help patients. However the claims made by the company were sky high, and if you read the patents – it's incredible some of them were granted with the science fiction like claims that they made – you would realize there was a lot of smoke and mirrors surrounding the company. Despite that many good people who had reached the top of their professions in politics or the military and business became so infatuated with the idea of a medical breakthrough that would "save lives" that they ignored the endless flashing of warning signals. In the end, Theranos was a bomb, and now, people are even facing prosecution.

Of course, that isn't to say that every novel idea is wrong. But you should apply two principles:

- Go into any investment with your eyes wide open. Be skeptical and don't ignore flashing warning signs. If the warning signs are flashing, there is a reason – and you should steer clear of the investment.
- If you do decide to invest in the next big thing – only invest a small portion of your overall capital. Remember all too often the next big thing fizzles. If you put all your money into something that ends up failing, you end up broke and back to square one. Don't be that person.

Falling in love with one company and failure to diversify

This mistake is closely related to the previous one, but can also take shape when we are talking about large, well-known companies. For example, as everyone knows, Apple has its so-called fanbois who love the company to the point of absurdity. It does have good products that sell of course, but when you love a company that much, it might cloud your investment decisions. Again, don't take it the wrong way – obviously, Apple has been a good investment decision for a lot of people – so it worked out. But it won't always work out, and as they say, nothing lasts forever. While we're confident Apple will be around for a very long time, it may not be as dominant in the future as it has been the past decade. And that lack of dominance means its stock will become lackluster. Not a loser, for sure, but it is not going to skyrocket like it did after the iPhone was released.

The point is you can invest in your favorite companies – hopefully, there isn't just one – but you're going to be far better off if that investment takes up a minority position in your portfolio. Remember that diversity is king. A suggestion would be to invest 20% in Apple and 80% in index funds.

Knowing when to let go

Sometimes you may have a favorite company, especially if it's a new and exciting one, and get so emotionally attached to it that you can't let go. That can be a huge mistake and cost a lot in losses if the company ends up going south. And that does happen from time to time. There are many companies at the time of writing – such as Tesla – that excite a lot of people with the possibilities, but the way Tesla is going to turn out is very uncertain. If you are really in love with the idea of electric cars and Tesla's style and potential – are you really going to be able to break from it if the promises don't materialize? If you see that after another year your investment isn't going anywhere, it might be time to move on. As with everything else, diversity helps. If you are a diversified, long-term investor, then no single company – even if you're putting significant sums into Apple and Tesla – is going to destroy your overall portfolio.

Too much turnover –trading too often

Some people think they can game the market. The most extreme example are day traders. If you fail to hold any stocks, you can put yourself at risk of never making any progress. Or you might make some money – but end up having a lot less money than you would have made had you simply followed a buy and hold strategy.

Bad market timing

Bad market timing might be the worse offense. Again, individual investors often sit on the sidelines. Then, after years of the stock market going up and up, they finally decide to get in. Then, a recession hits. That is bad market timing. They might find themselves in a buy high sell low situation. Using a dollar cost averaging strategy can help you avoid this.

CHAPTER 9
International Investing

For those who are more ambitious, international investing beckons. There has never been a better time for international investing, as the old standby markets are still going strong – the United Kingdom, the EU, Canada, Australia, and Japan – there are also great opportunities in emerging markets. The emerging markets are beginning to enter a more mature phase, but there is still an enormous amount of room for massive growth in the coming decades. Also, newer emerging markets will be developing in countries that may not have been favorable in the past.

Is international investing for you

Who is international investing good for? Practically any investor. However, in general, if you are more comfortable with risk, you'll be better suited for international investing.

However, international investing is not entirely risky. Obviously, the world abounds with mature and safe markets outside the United States such as in Britain, Europe, and Japan.

For emerging markets, there are tools available that can also help you mitigate risk. The best way for investors, especially beginners, to get involved in investing in emerging markets is through mutual funds or exchange-traded funds.

The risks of international investing

One of the main risks encountered in international investing is liquidity risk. This is the risk that you can't convert a security into cash in a timely fashion. Or, you may not be able to convert a security into cash without incurring a loss.

Translated that means you might have a stock you want to sell in an international market, but you're unable to sell it as quickly as you'd like. That can mean either having to sell it at a loss or having to hold onto it when you need to get rid of it.

Many foreign markets will have lower trading volumes, and they may also not be open all day long in smaller markets. That makes selling stock more difficult.

A second risk you will face – if directly buying foreign stocks on foreign markets – is currency risk. In order to buy something overseas, you have to trade your U.S. dollars for the currency of the other country, and then buy the asset. Exchange rates between different currencies are fluctuating daily, and this can impact your investment decisions.

Currency volatility can impact the value of stocks in unforeseen ways. You don't know what the exchange rates are going to be three months, six months, or a year down the road. So directly investing in foreign markets carries added risk, in that you've got to worry not only·about the performance of the stock – but also worry about currency volatility. This can be very difficult for beginning investors to deal with. Experienced investors will know how to hedge the currency risk, which is an investment used to mitigate the risk of currency fluctuations.

Another risk is that foreign markets might have higher transaction costs.

Lack of information can also be a risk for those investing in foreign markets, and it's another issue that can be very impactful for beginning investors. The United States and other countries like Great Britain have strictly enforced regulations that require companies to provide certain transparent information that will help investors make decisions that are in their best interests. Many emerging markets may not have the same level of transparency, and in some countries, a company prospectus may not even be available in English. If you don't know what you are doing, then you might not make the best decisions.

Another obvious problem is political and social stability. The world is not always at peace, and sometimes, governments fall apart, or wars happen. This can make investing risky. If there is a major collapse or a war you might not be able to unload your investments. And while things may seem fine at the time you make your investments, none of us can see the future, so the risk is always there.

Next, another risk you may face is legal remedies. If you get in trouble when dealing with a company in the United States, you have access to U.S. courts where you can seek redress or a settlement. If you're investing in a foreign country, you may lack access to the courts to be able to seek a remedy. Even if you do have access, it goes without saying that all court systems are not created equal.

Traditional overseas markets

By "traditional," we mean long-term developed markets. Overseas markets that might meet this definition include:

- Great Britain
- The European Union
- Australia and New Zealand
- Hong Kong
- South Korea
- Japan
- Canada

Investing in emerging markets

Emerging markets are far riskier for a whole host of reasons, from problematic court systems to political instability to liquidity problems. That said, many emerging markets offer the promise of high returns. Some emerging markets of interest include:

- China
- Brazil
- India
- Vietnam

- South Africa

How to invest in overseas markets

The first way to invest in overseas markets is actually to trade on the foreign markets themselves. Doing so will incur all of the risks that we discussed above. You may be able to find a broker who can help you proceed this way, but it is not recommended for beginning investors.

Seeking the advice of the United States government, we've identified the safest ways to invest in overseas markets. The most straightforward way is to seek out overseas companies that trade directly in U.S. stock markets. You can visit the New York Stock Exchange website where you can obtain lists of foreign companies that are traded on the NYSE, which gives you opportunities to invest in foreign companies with some reduction in risk directly. Doing it this way is quite different than trying to buy stocks on a foreign exchange. You can visit the site here:

https://www.nyse.com/listings/international-listings

According to the SEC, most foreign companies trade in the United States using a tool called the American Depository Receipt or ADR. An ADR allows you to purchase the representation of a share of foreign stock, and an ADR is priced at the price of the stock in its home market. ADRs that trade in the United States can be purchased through a broker.

The best way to invest overseas is...surprise – mutual funds and exchange-traded funds. There are many available funds that invest in foreign markets – but you have the professionals setting them up for you and taking care of the risks. You can invest right at home, completely shielded from many of the problems that foreign investing entails. Just like any other mutual fund or exchange-traded fund, you can invest in them as if they are a stock index or other type of fund.

Let's look at a few options. Since we prefer exchange-traded funds, we will look at those, but if you'd prefer a mutual fund, you will find similar funds you can invest in taking that route.

We will go back to State Street Global Advisors (SPDR), but you can find similar funds on your favorite exchange-traded fund website. The first thing we will note is that there are global funds for every available market. Better and larger markets tend to be singled out for investment, while others are grouped together into single funds. Individual countries you can target with a State Street ETF include:

- China
- United Kingdom
- Japan
- Hong Kong
- Germany
- Canada

You can also invest in the "Global DOW" index, which tracks 150 international companies (including top U.S. companies) that the Wall Street Journal and others have selected as the world's 150 top companies.

Other options include:

- Investing in Europe (a fund that invests in Europe as a whole)
- Asia/Pacific emerging markets
- Developed world
- International small cap

If you look at iShares, you can find more targeted options. For example, they have funds that allow you to invest in:

- Taiwan
- South Korea
- Brazil

- Russia
- Malaysia
- South Africa
- Saudi Arabia
- China
- India

And many more.

What we've found is that international investing is entirely accessible using ETFs and you will find it's the same for mutual funds. You can select targeted or broad investments, and since you're using a U.S. traded fund, you've got a lot more protection than if you tried to do it alone. If you are looking to invest in specific international companies, you are best off seeking out international companies that are foreign based but trading on the New York Stock Exchange.

CHAPTER 10
Bonds And Government Securities

Bonds are a form of debt, with the investor playing the role of a bank. Bonds are issued by a wide variety of entities, from municipal governments to corporations. The most famous bonds are those issued by the United States federal government. In this chapter, we will give an overview of bonds and how they work.

Bonds in detail

When you take out a loan, the bank gives you a sum of cash. You make payments on the loan, which will include paying some of the principal back with interest. A bond is a form of a loan, but instead of banks making the loan, investors loan the money. They don't work exactly like the type of loans you are used to; however, because the entity issuing the bond doesn't pay back the principal until the end of the life of the bond. And of course, if you want a car loan, you don't issue bonds to the bank.

Bonds are used to raise cash. A government may need cash for a wide variety of needs. Local governments can issue bonds to build roads, repair school buildings, or build new county hospitals. Typically the bonds are voted on in local elections, and if voters approve the municipality will issue bonds to investors. Historically, municipal bonds have been a favored investment used by the wealthy, since they provide a tax shelter in addition to providing regular interest payments, hence generating income.

The federal government has used bonds, called U.S. Treasuries, to find budget shortfalls. As everyone knows by now, the U.S. government is in massive debt and yet continues to spend more money than it takes in – so it's continually issuing new bonds. Since their inception, bonds issued by the U.S. government have been considered to be extremely reliable, if not perfectly reliable. They are backed by "the full faith and credit of the United States." Even with the large debts the U.S. government has amassed, people worldwide remain confident in U.S. Treasuries and continue to invest in them.

The federal government also issues bonds to raise money for emergencies, in particular for wars. U.S. Savings bonds and liberty bonds are two well-known examples.

Corporations also issue bonds. They are often issued by top companies like Apple, Ford, and IBM. When you buy one of these bonds, you're lending the company money, so it is not the same as a stock investment. If you invest in a bond issued by Apple, you have no ownership interest in the company. Apple will pay you interest payments on a regular basis, but when the bond is up (the 'maturity date'), Apple will return your principal.

Some bonds carry more risk than others. For example, there might be bonds issued by companies that have a bad history when it comes to paying the money back. These are called "junk bonds," and because of the higher risk associated with investing in junk bonds, higher interest rates have to be paid. In recent times, some government entities are running into trouble meeting their obligations. On the opposite end of the spectrum from junk bonds that pay high yields or interest rates but carry a risk that you'll lose the principal (or that at some point they won't make the interest payment), are investment-grade bonds, issued by those with a solid record of paying their interest rates and returning the principal.

Bonds are considered relatively safe. In the stock market, in theory, you could lose everything. Generally speaking, that isn't true with bonds since they are required to pay back your principal. For this reason, they are considered a safe investment. Although some governments are running into financial trouble, the taxation power of governments ensures that the investor has high confidence in the government paying back the principal on any bonds it issues.

Now let's familiarize ourselves with some jargon used when discussing bonds:

- Maturity: this is the end date of the bond. When the maturity date is reached, the principal must be paid back in full.
- Par Value: Also known as face value, this is the value of the bond when it's issued by the company or government. It is also the amount of principal you must invest in taking hold of the bond. The par value is noted because bonds often trade on markets after they are issued. Prices of bonds will rise and fall based on prevailing interest rates. If the bonds price on the market is less than the par value, then it's a discount. If the bonds price on the market is higher than the par value, it's a premium. If you buy a bond directly from the issuing entity when it's issued, then you will pay the par value.
- Coupon: This is the interest rate or yield on the bond. Yield is given as a percentage of par value. If you have a $1,000 bond with a 7% yield, then it will pay an interest payment of $70. Yields can be fixed rate, in which case the rate is constant over the lifetime of the bond, or they can be variable. Variable interest rates are pegged as a spread to some measures in the economy, such as the LIBOR rate which is a rate charged for interbank lending.
- Default Risk: the risk that the principal won't be paid back.
- Callable: A bond that can be called by the issuer at a date prior to the maturity date. Of course, if a bond is called, they have to pay back the principal. Since the issuer can call the bond at any time, the investor assumes more risk, and interest rates on callable bonds are higher.
- Putable: If a bond is putable, the buyer/investor can force the issuer to pay back the principal before the maturity date. Yields for putable bonds are lower.
- Convertible: A type of corporate bond, which can be converted into common stock at a later date. These bonds have a conversion rate, which is the number of shares the investor gets in exchange for converting the bond to stock. Convertible bonds pay lower interest rates. If the price of the shares that is equal to the conversion rate is greater than the par value of the bond, then it's to the advantage of the

investors to convert the bond. If it's lower, then the investor would be doing a losing deal. When it's equal to the par value, then that is the breakeven price.

- Asset-Backed Securities: Bonds created that bundle together income streams from assets into a bond.

Corporate bonds – how they work

All bonds work in the same way, so corporate bonds work as described in the previous section. However, since many corporate bonds can carry risk, it's important to know what the risk categories are.

- Highest Quality: Rated AAA by S&P/Fitch, and Aaa by Moody's. These are investment grade bonds. Investors can be confident they will get their principal back and that the issuer will not default on interest payments.
- High Quality: Rated AA by S&P/Fitch and Aa by Moody's. Also investment grade.
- Strong: Rated A by all credit agencies. Riskier, but still investment grade. Will have to pay higher interest rates.
- Medium Grade: Rated BBB by S&P/Fitch and Baa by Moody's. Still investment grade, but higher risk than strong, so will pay higher interest rates.
- Speculative: Rated BB, B by S&P/Fitch and Ba, B by Moody's. Junk bonds. These have some risk of default. They have to pay higher interest rates than any of the above.
- Highly Speculative: Rated CCC/CC/C by S&P/Fitch and Caa, Ca, C by Moody's. Invest at your own risk. Very risky Junk bonds but will pay higher interest rates.
- In Default: Rated D by S&P/Fitch and C by Moody's- the lowest of the junk bonds.

Beginning investors probably shouldn't invest in junk bonds, but there are reasons that speculators do so. The first is to receive high-interest rate payments. Also if the issuer of the bond gets its act together – in part by keeping up with interest payments and improving its rating – then the bond can be sold to another investor at a value that is higher than the par value, giving the speculator a profit. These are high-risk activities with little certainty built into them, so that is why we refer to "speculator" rather than an investor.

Bond Pricing

Bonds are bought and sold on secondary markets but not at their par value. Bond prices move inversely with interest rates. So after a bond is issued, if the interest rate goes up, the older bond isn't worth as much. So it will sell for a price below its par value, or at a discount. For example, if you buy a $10,000 bond with a coupon rate of 4%, which means you will receive a $400 interest payment every year. However, suppose interest rates go up and now the company issues bonds that have a 6% coupon rate. Now, someone can buy a new bond that will pay them $600 a year – so your bond is less desirable and so if you sell it on the market it has to be sold at a discount.

On the other hand, if interest rates drop, that makes the previously issued bond more valuable. Suppose that you buy a $10,000 bond that pays 5% interest, or $500 per year. Then, interest rates crater to 3%, so new $10,000 bonds that are being issued only pay $300 a year. That makes your bond a desirable investment, and investors will bid up the price and be willing to pay more than the par value to get a higher interest rate. In that case, you can sell more than the par value at a premium.

Zero coupon securities

Some bonds are known as zero-coupon bonds or zero-coupon securities. This is a bond which makes no interest payments. Zero coupon bonds are sold at large discounts from the par value. However, the value of the bond appreciates and can be redeemed at face value on the maturity date. This enables the investor who buys the bond to make a profit even though no interest is paid.

What are municipal bonds

Municipal bonds, which are usually called "munis," are issued by state and local governments. Typically they are used to fund capital projects like the construction of a prison, bridge, or library. Municipal bonds are exempt from federal taxes, and often from state taxes as well. As such they have long been used to shelter income from taxation. While government bonds are backed by the taxation power of the issuer, that power isn't unlimited and not all municipal bonds have top ratings. However, some are backed by insurance companies.

Treasuries: Investing in the US government

There are several types of bonds available from the Federal government:

- Treasury Bills or T-Bills: These are short term, with maturity dates ranging from a few weeks up to 26 weeks. The face value is $1,000, but they are sold at a discount and redeemed at face value. There are no interest payments, the difference between what you receive when the bond is redeemed and what you paid at a discount is the interest.
- Treasury notes: these are longer term, available in two-, five-, and ten-year issues. They are issued in increments of $1,000.
- Treasury Bonds: These are 30-year notes. Interest is paid every six months until the maturity date.
- TIPS: These are inflation-protected bonds. They pay lower interest rates, but the interest rate and principal are both routinely adjusted for inflation.
- Savings Bonds: Can be redeemed at any point one year after bond issue. Earn small interest payment every six months which is saved until you redeem the bond. Issued in increments from $50 to $10,000. When purchased, they are sold for half of the par value, so you can purchase a $10,000 bond for $5,000. Those purchased online are purchased at face value but start at half the amount ($25). You can hold a savings bond for 30 years. When you redeem the bond, then you get the accrued interest plus your initial investment back.

- I-Bonds: A type of savings bond adjusted for inflation every six months. They pay interest which is adjusted for inflation.

Advantages and Pitfalls of government securities

Government bonds offer some extra security and some tax advantages. Despite growing problems with debt people remain confident in the U.S. government and still confident in less secure state and local bonds. The tax advantages of munis are an attractive feature of these bonds. However as governments become more and more in debt the attractiveness of government-issued bonds will begin decreasing at some point, although nobody knows when that will happen.

How to Invest

You can buy bonds from a brokerage. Some brokerages are municipal security dealers. You can buy treasuries directly from the federal government. Bonds can also be bought and sold on secondary markets, including through your own personal investment account that you self-manage.

And as usual, you can invest in bonds through either a mutual fund or an ETF.

CHAPTER 11
Playing It Safe With Banking

At the root of the financial system are the banks, and although interest rates have been very low for many years now, many people still find banks appealing for the perceived safety of preserving cash.

Banking in an era of low interest rates

Low-interest rates can be an issue when interest rates are so low that they are not outstripped by inflation. In that case, you have to weigh keeping money in the bank against losing its value through inflation. Obviously, you need to keep some money in the bank for emergencies. Other assets like stock are not as liquid (meaning not as easily converted into cash). However, while in the past people might have loaded up savings accounts and CDs, doing so at the present time is of questionable value. You should keep a savings account that has enough cash in it for immediate emergencies, but having a $250,000 savings account that is barely keeping up with inflation – or even losing value – is not the best idea. Check current interest rates to evaluate this situation.

Money Market Accounts and Funds

A money market account will come with a higher interest rate than a standard savings account. However, it will also have a higher balance and deposit requirements. At the time of writing, even with higher interest rates, money market accounts are only paying around 2%. They also allow debit cards and checks but place a limit of 6 debit card charges and six checks per month.

A money market fund is a mutual fund or ETF that invests in cash. It invests directly in cash, in cash equivalent securities, CDs, and debt-based securities with short term maturity dates. Unlike a Money Market Account, which is an FDIC insured bank account, a money market fund is the same as any other fund – so it does not guarantee principal although they are considered low-risk investments. Money market funds also invest in U.S. Treasuries. You can buy and sell shares of money market funds just like any other mutual fund or ETF.

What is a CD

A CD is a certificate of deposit. They are risk-free investments since they are insured by the FDIC. They are sold by banks, thrifts, and credit unions. Typically, they are held for 1, 3, or 5 years. They may require a minimum deposit, and the longer they are held, the higher the interest rate paid. Some are topping 3 % at the time of writing, which is better but still barely above inflation.

Are banks still worth it?

The answer is yes. Banks still provide a means to access money for day-to-day spending activities and a way to save money. Also while interest rates are low now, there is no reason to expect that to be permanent.

CHAPTER 12
The Investing Mindset

Investing involves some risk. Many of us have been raised to avoid risk. Overcoming that fear of risk is important for the investing mindset.

The mindset of the investor

Getting into the proper mindset of the investor means being willing to accept some level of risk – but also taking steps to mitigate risk. Simply jumping into risky situations is reckless. The investor accepts risk but does not act in a reckless fashion. When possible, the investor looks for ways to hedge or reduce their risks.

Getting into the investing mindset

I grew up in an era when people had parents that had lived through the great depression. The experience of the great depression had a negative impact on many people that discouraged the investor mindset. The 2008 financial crisis had the same impact.

To help get in the investing mindset, you can take practical, and mental/spiritual steps. Taking some practical steps can help you feel more secure and better able to handle risks. Ideally, it will set you up so that if you take a big hit in the market, you will remain basically OK in a stable situation, and not facing ruin or bankruptcy. Some steps you can take include:

• Before you invest a large amount of money, build up your savings, or if you have none open a savings account. Save 3-6 months' worth of money and leave it in the account. Pledge never to touch it and don't use it to bail out your investments – it's for living expenses and emergencies only.
• Start investing small. When you invest small amounts in the beginning, you will increase your comfort level slowly.
• Engage in affirmations. Train your mind to be comfortable with risk and investing.

- Study how investors used hedges to "hedge their bets," that is reduce risk.

What level of investing is for you

At first, a deep level of investing might not be in your interest. Your level of investing can increase with time.

CHAPTER 13
Retirement Vehicles

We've discussed some of these items earlier, but let's have a look at the definitions of options available to build retirement funds. Of course any investment functions in part as a retirement fund.

401k and other employer-based plans

A 401k is a type of employer managed investment plan. Generally speaking, they have replaced pensions in an era when people don't stick to one employer for their entire working life and pensions became too expensive to manage. A 401k lets you make any type of investment, including stocks, bonds, mutual funds, or ETFs and cash investments. You can work with a 401k in the same way you would with any investment plan, and probably receive matching from your employer.

Traditional IRA

As noted earlier, an IRA is an individual retirement account. They have some tax advantages. You can invest up to $5,500 per year, but after age 50 the IRS allows you to make larger contributions. With a traditional IRA, you get a tax deduction on the invested money now but will have to pay taxes when the money is withdrawn. An IRA is an account, so can have multiple securities in it of various types.

Roth IRA

A Roth IRA is similar to a traditional IRA; however, the money you put in is taxed now. When you withdraw it after retirement, it is tax-free. Roth IRAs, however, have some income limitations.

Annuities

An annuity is basically an income stream provided by an insurance company. You invest money with them and receive a fixed payment each month in return. The payment is for life; however, you and your heirs will not have access to the principal once you enter into the annuity.

529 College savings plans

There are college savings plans that work similar to other investment accounts, but you can only use the money to pay for college for your children. The accounts take advantage of the power of the market to raise funds.

Using your investments: when to start making withdrawals, and how much

The favored rule of thumb is you can withdraw 4% of your total investments per year. So, if you have $100,000 (hopefully it's a lot more), then you could safely withdraw $4,000 per year. So if you want to have an income of $100,000 a year in retirement, you'll need $2,500,000.

CHAPTER 14
Advanced Techniques

We've already discussed these topics throughout some of the earlier chapters, but we have gathered the advanced topics here together briefly for a centralized reference. A word of caution – using these techniques can be downright dangerous, making you completely broke or in a spiral of debt.

What is Options trading

An option is a contract that governs the buying and selling of a security. It allows an investor to either buy or sell the security at a predetermined price. So the price is set regardless of what happens to the price of the asset before the maturity date for the contract. It is called an option because this is an option for the investor; they are allowed to make the deal but aren't required to. Options contracts are actually bought and sold themselves on markets where investors do options trading.

Calls

A call is a type of options contract. In a call, the buyer has the right to purchase, but not the obligation, securities at an agreed-upon price on a certain date. The buyer pays a fee to the seller called a premium. The seller must sell to the buyer, even if the price that has been agreed to is lower than the price of the security at the time of the sale.

Puts

A put is the inverse of a call, in that the option now rests with the seller. In a put contract, the seller has the right to sell, but not the obligation, securities at a predetermined price on a specific date. A put option is used to protect stock against falling prices.

Strike Price

The price agreed upon for a call or a put.

Margin Trading

When trading on the margin, the brokerage lends the investor money to buy securities. The investor has to pay the brokerage back the money. High requirements are set for margin trading, and it can be dangerous. Trading on the margin got a lot of investors in trouble when the Great Depression hit.

Day Trading

Day trading involves buying and selling stocks on the same day, with the goal of making short term profits. Day traders often sit at their computers all day long trading stocks. Day trading can be lucrative for experienced investors that know what they are doing. If you are a stock market beginner, you should probably gain a lot of experience buying stocks and studying the markets before embarking on day trading.

CHAPTER 15
How To Invest Large Sums Of Money

Investing large sums of money isn't really any different than investing $100. The same principles apply. Namely, you want to use dollar cost averaging and diversification while choosing specific investment types that help you meet your desired goals. Remember that the risk of losing your principal is always there.

Going all in

Going all in is a bad idea. If you do so with a large sum of money, then your risks are magnified. You can review the common mistakes discussed earlier in the book to go over the details again, but going all in puts you at risk of bad market timing, buying high right before a downturn, and so on.

Going slow, building over time

Although it is tempting to put $100,000 or a million dollars right into the markets if you've not been in stocks before, it is better to follow the dollar cost averaging strategy. You should divide up the money you are going to invest into monthly payments to be invested over a fairly large time period, say 3-5 years. This will help you avoid the mistakes that arise from the volatility of the market.

Second, you should implement the diversity principles outlined in the book. In addition to investing in a wide variety of stocks and possibly foreign markets, take advantage of the fact that when investing a large sum you also have the opportunity to hold some in reserve with money market funds, and can also invest a lot in the bond markets. You may invest a large amount in bonds, and the percentage will depend on your growth goals, but note that with large amounts to invest after you learn the markets you can profit from bond trading as well.

Dangers of investing large sums

The same dangers exist that exist for all other investing. Mainly you're risking wasting money buying high and being forced to sell low, or buying at the top of the market right before a bear market hits – causing you to miss out on low-cost buying opportunities. If you are investing slowly and regularly, when the bear market arrives, you'll be in a position to take advantage of it because you will have capital available for the buying opportunities. If you go all in you might not have it readily available if it's available at all – in fact, it won't be. You will have to sell your own securities at discounts. Also, avoid the emotional panic that sets in and causes people to bail from the markets when they should ride it out. Selling a large amount at a loss to stuff it in the bank for a temporary downturn is a bad approach.

Reducing your risks

If you are a large investor, rather than going it alone, you should seek out the advice of an advisor. You don't even need the advisor to make the investments and can run a self-directed account if that is your desire, but you should talk to a professional about hedging your risks. You don't want to get too anxious and make newbie mistakes that might cost you a large sum of money you currently have access too. Having a large amount of money will actually give you access to financial tools to hedge your risks, and you should talk to a professional about how to do this.

CONCLUSION

Congratulations on making it to the end of this book. We hope that you have enjoyed it and learned a great deal about investing and the options that are available to you! If you found this book useful, we hope that you will take the time to rate the book!

Now is the time for action. It is one thing to learn about investing and the stock market, but if you take no action, you will make no progress. Find the right kinds of investments that meet your goals. If you want to protect the money that you already have, then some mix of bonds, savings accounts, and a smaller level of investment in safer stocks will be in your interest.

If you don't have much money saved and need to grow cash for retirement or want to retire early, then a more aggressive portfolio is in your interest. In that case, while you'll want to use some indexed funds for some protection while still getting good levels of growth, you will also want to invest aggressively in smaller companies and emerging markets.

Whatever path you choose, we thank you again and wish you the best of luck!

CPSIA information can be obtained
at www.ICGtesting.com
Printed in the USA
BVHW041402240521
607999BV00005B/1101